Powerless No Longer

Powerless No Longer

Reprogramming Your Addictive Behavior

Independently Published by

Peter W. Soderman

Independently Published 2013 with CreateSpace by Peter W. Soderman

First Edition August, 2013

ISBN-13: 978-1492185895
ISBN-10: 1492185892

Dewey Decimal: 616.8606

Cover art by Dan Ray Davie

For recovering addicts everywhere

And

For Judith

We cannot solve our problems with the same thinking we used when we created them.
-Albert Einstein

Contents

Foreword

If you are reading this book, there is a good chance you have fears. You may have fears that you have tried before to overcome your addiction and you will fail again. You may have fears that addictions are mysterious things and that you are somehow irretrievably different from "normal" people. You may fear that even if you remain sober, you will be in continual pain and "white knuckling" it. You may fear that you are doomed to failure. This book by Pete Soderman will show you how to overcome these fears and indeed errors and will show you the path toward building your life back again.

Much of the perceived wisdom about addictions is just wrong. Pete brings an evidence based approach both to why addictions occur and how to get over them. There are powerful new understandings of both the cause and the cure of additive behaviors and this book clearly explains them. Addictions are not mysterious behaviors anymore, but well understood natural processes.

Pete also has personal insights into the recovery process with a deep compassion for those suffering. He has walked out of the shadows and slavery of addiction and into the light of sobriety himself. He demystifies what happens to you when you become addicted. He presents proven tools that work to help you regain control, gain sobriety, and rebalance your life. Using those tools is still up to you, but using them will make your recovery easier, surer and set you up for success for the long haul, not just day at a time. You will find that the distortions in your thinking can be changed. You can get off of "automatic pilot" and regain the values that make life rich and fulfilling.   Use what he has shared here and believe you can recover, can restore meaning and purpose in your life, and move beyond your addictive behavior to a better life.

Michael Werner
cognitive recovery pioneer

Acknowledgements

First of all, I would like to thank the thousands of dedicated researchers who continue to push back the wall of ignorance, superstition, and fear surrounding addiction. If it weren't for their tireless efforts, we would still be locking addicts away in institutions, instead of finding ever more efficacious ways to help them recover.

I am indebted to a number of people, beginning with my friend Mike Werner, who first acquainted me with SMART Recovery®, and gave me the initial idea for *Powerless*. My daughter Judith, the catalyst for my personal *Crystallization of Discontent,* who nine months later loved me enough to give me permission to do what she knew I needed to do in spite of the impact it would have on her own life. My wife and best friend, Gethyn, who found me all those years ago, and for some reason, had faith in me. Thank you for putting-up with this book's extended gestation period.

Thanks to my friend, Dan Ray Davie, who did the artwork for the front cover.

Special thanks to three friends here in Ajijic, who spent their own time pouring over the manuscript, culling-out countless commas, and eliminating many affronts to conventions of grammar and style. Susana Douglas, Joy Dunstan, and Brenda Dawson, you have my heartfelt thanks.

Finally, to all those I have met on my recovery journey, this is your story too because I have learned from each and every one of you. Thank you for being there.

Introduction

In the fall of 2009, my friend Mike Werner showed me a copy of *The Craving Brain*, by Ronald A. Ruden. On page 101 was a diagram labeled "The Craving Response for Alcohol." At the top of the diagram was a stimulus, in this case a jingle of ice cubes, leading to a "Pattern Recognition and Perception" phase, followed by a "Landscape" phase, where such things as stress level, serotonin level and other forces came into play.

Next was the "Craving Response" phase, where rising levels of dopamine would drive the addict in one of two possible directions: either into the arms of Alcoholics Anonymous, or towards a first drink. The AA branch would lead to a conditioned rise of serotonin, followed by the ability to abstain. The other branch, of course, would lead to continued drinking.

Near the top of the diagram, on the same level as the stimulus, was a note: "Buddhism acts here," with an arrow pointing to the "Pattern Recognition" phase. The implication was that Buddhism short-circuited the craving response because it relieved the practitioner of their conditioned mental attitudes and belief systems. I remember saying to Mike, "Wow, SMART Recovery® acts exactly the same way, somebody should write a book explaining why."

Mike's response was, "Why don't you," and that was the beginning of *Powerless No Longer*.

SMART, which stands for Self-Management and Recovery Training, is the leading self-empowering addiction recovery group, with meetings all over the world. SMART teaches a set of evidence-based recovery tools based upon the latest scientific research.

When I began with SMART, I didn't know why it worked; I just knew that it did. It resonated with me right from the beginning. It just made sense, in a way that no other recovery program ever had, including Alcoholics Anonymous.

In my early years in recovery, AA taught me not to question the tenets of the program. "There *is* no chapter called "why it works," I was told, so don't worry about it. That would have been fine if it *did* work, but it became obvious to me after a few years that it *didn't* work, at least not for most people. Some recovered of course, but the vast majority struggled with their addictions for years.

Why was that? Why was it that some people just couldn't stay sober, while others seemed to "get it" and quit almost effortlessly? What did they know that the rest didn't? Why did recovery seem to be more about changing thoughts and beliefs than working steps, praying, and going to meetings for the rest of your life?

I had lots of questions, and very few answers. In the beginning, I was just out to satisfy my own intellectual curiosity. I never really thought I could produce something like what you hold in your hand (or in your electronic reading device). I didn't think I was capable, I certainly didn't have the credentials, and I never thought I could stick with the project until the end. In spite of all of that, here it is.

I facilitate a SMART Recovery® meeting, but I do not speak for the organization. The comments and opinions in *Powerless No Longer* are mine alone, and do not necessarily reflect those of SMART Recovery®. SMART and other programs that offer evidence-based solutions use many of the tools and methods discussed in *Powerless*. I have just gathered in one place all of the tools that seem to work for most people, along with the evidence that supports them. The research proves that these tools and methods can help you recover from virtually any addictive substance or behavior, as long as you are willing to do a little work.

The research that constitutes the backbone of this book is available to anyone with a computer and an internet connection. Most of the references in the endnotes are scientific research papers written by experts in the field, and you can read them for yourself. Please don't be put off by their presence. They are there as a starting point for those who would like to go a little further in their study of addiction.

You may notice that much of the narrative in *Powerless* seems geared to dependence upon alcohol. This should come as no surprise, as alcohol is overwhelmingly the drug of choice among addicted Americans. According to the latest National Survey on Drug Use and Health, of the 22 million people classified with substance dependence or abuse, over 80% were addicted to alcohol. Please do not assume that the tools and techniques explained in this book will not work for other addictions or behaviors because the studies show that they do. For those familiar with AA and its derivatives, I can assure you that addiction does not recognize any "singleness of purpose." The irrational beliefs that perpetuate our misery are virtually the same across the board.

I am not out to save the world, I don't think I have discovered a "better way," or that I have the only ticket to recovery. *Powerless No Longer* is not a silver bullet, guaranteed to remove your addiction or double your money back. There *is* no such thing. The good news is that there are many paths to recovery; the bad news is that every single one of them requires effort on your part.

My job is to tell you a little about your addiction, starting with how it came to be, and what you can do about it. I will introduce you to the methods that have the widest evidentiary support, and show you not just how, but also why they work. You will learn a little about how your brain functions, how it got the way it is, and how you can reprogram it to overcome any addictive behavior.

What's your job? Well, that's really what it's all about, isn't it? What happens next is up to you. I will show you that you are not powerless over your addiction, and that means that *you* are responsible for your own outcome. If you think that puts the focus upon you, congratulations, you are beginning to understand.

Chapter 1: The End of a Long Nightmare

The last night

One night in late August, 1990, I was sitting in my living room, continuing a normal evening of drinking, after the mosquitoes drove me inside. I was making up stories in my head about adventures that would never happen, when my fifteen-year-old daughter appeared out of nowhere. She stood ten feet in front of me, fiddling with a piece of paper in her hand.

"Dad," she said with a tremor in her voice, "what did you think of the poem I read for you on the deck? You said you wanted to think about it for a while."

"What poem?" I couldn't remember even seeing her earlier, let alone any poem.

Thrusting the paper towards me, she said, "This poem, Dad. I've been working on it for days."

I looked towards the floor and muttered something, hoping it was appropriate. I can't remember what I said. When our eyes met, I watched her expression change from hurt to anger, then from anger to disgust. I saw myself reflected in her eyes, as we both realized at the same instant that I was a complete fraud.

She crumpled the paper into a ball and tossed it onto the rug. Her hair swirled as she spun on her heel and ran from the room. I forgot the poem, but I still remember her sobs.

I looked around the room as if seeing it for the first time, and realized this was coming to an end and damn soon. We were living off sales from two years ago, and the pipeline was empty. I was a liar, a cheat, and a phony, and one of the few around me who didn't realize it.

If the world would stop, I thought, I could get myself together, and begin to make things right. I tried hard not to drink any more that evening, but the glass magically continued to fill itself. When the pendulum clock on the wall bonged 1 AM, I stumbled up the stairs, undressed, and fell into bed. As the room began to spin, I felt absolute panic. I knew I couldn't face life without alcohol to kill the pain, yet I knew I would die if I continued to drink. I saw no third option.

The nature of addiction

Addicts are not much different from anyone else; we've just learned to see the world from a distorted perspective. We have learned to be addicts. Genetics play a role, but we weren't born with our addictions, nor did we acquire them due to a moral flaw or shortcoming. Addiction is a complex bio/psycho/social disorder with many different causes. It's a continuum, meaning there are degrees of addiction; it's not an on-or-off condition. Addiction makes irreversible changes to the brain that can become so severe that the only help available to the addict are programs that feature harm reduction, like methadone or needle exchange.

The last five years of my drinking career were by far the worst. I was failing at work, my personal life was a mess, and I got into one scrape after another. I was doing the kinds of things that hurt people, ruin reputations, and cause pain to everyone involved. Alcohol relieved the pain, but it was while drinking that I did things that caused it and so on, and so on.... One day, I reached the point where alcohol no longer dulled the pain, at least while I was conscious, but I continued to drink. I had to. When I drank enough, it produced the relief of oblivion. It didn't start out that way; it took me twenty-six years of slow, almost unnoticeable progression to reach that point.

We become addicts by using sufficient quantities of certain substances for enough time to develop changes in our brains, affecting both our physiology and our perceptions of reality. At first we use because we receive positive feedback—it makes us feel good—like one of the gang. We learn to use it to feel better about ourselves, and make that not quite good enough feeling disappear. As social drug users, we're sure we have a handle on life. Using helps us cope with the stresses we face when interacting with others. For some of us, it makes us feel we could walk through walls. For others, it adds that layer of insulation that seems to protect everyone else from life's unpleasant moments.

We hardly notice that after a while it takes more and more of the substance to make us comfortable with the world. Although using more, we are still able to choose whether to have a glass of wine or help a child with their homework. We can stop after "one or two" if we face an important meeting at work, or we are driving our family somewhere for an outing. We may occasionally binge, as our drug-seeking habits become more ingrained, but we are still making socially appropriate, conscious choices.

If we continue on this path long enough, we lose the ability to make conscious choices about the amounts we use. Even after a period of abstinence, environmental cues or stressors can trigger drug use, hijacking our basic survival instincts, and triggering responses over which we have little control. Social concerns lose their meaning, no matter how pressing they are. We have learned we must have the drug, no matter what the cost, even to those we hold dear because we believe our basic survival is at stake. Family, job, possessions, and even personal safety are unimportant now. The drug is what matters.

Sounds hopeless, doesn't it? If it were, the addicts we will study in the next chapter wouldn't have been able to overcome their problem on their own, and I wouldn't be here. Not all of us experience the horrors in the last paragraph before something, a set of circumstances, causes us to focus on and question our drug use. The good news is the overwhelming majority of us overcome our addictions on our own without treatment centers, formal programs, pills, or patches. We can change the habits that created the addiction, and learn new skills to cope with the stresses that helped drive many of us to dependency in the first place. I never made it to the street, and you don't have to either.

Why me, and what's in it for you

You probably noticed that there are no letters after my name. I'm not a Ph.D., a psychiatrist, neurologist, therapist, or drug and alcohol counselor. In fact, I have a computer engineering background. I'm just an ordinary guy who was willing to do a great deal of research into an area in which I have a vested interest. *Powerless No Longer* is the result of two years of research, and over twenty years of observing and working with recovering addicts.

Professionals in the field, each of whom is eager to advance their own particular theory or method, dominate the recovery genre. My perspective is unique, in that I didn't start with the addicted population that shows up in hospitals and treatment centers. I started with the majority of addicts who recover on their own, and went searching for the evidence that tells us how they did it.

It is not necessary to understand how a computer works in order to send an email to a friend, or even to tell someone how to do it. Science may never completely understand addiction, but that doesn't mean we can't discover the best current methods to recover from it—and tell others about it.

If you are questioning your own drug or alcohol use, or have tried 12-step programs and not succeeded, *Powerless No Longer* is for you. If you believe you are "powerless" over your addiction, I will show that this is not true. I will describe the self-change methods that work for the addicts who recover on their own, and show you how to apply these principles in your own recovery. I have combined in one place:

- A detailed explanation of the bio/psycho/social aspects of addiction

- The research and studies that show how most people recover

- A comprehensive review of current recovery methods, and

- Suggestions you can use to take what's available and build a recovery program that fits your own needs

I will make suggestions based upon the available science; there are no "musts" in this book. No single program will work for everyone. Is *Powerless No Longer* a silver bullet? No, it is not. It will not cure your addiction, get your job back, or return your wife, your children, your husband, or your dog.

What it will do is give you an opportunity to see behind your behavior, and understand what motivates you. It will explain how addictive behaviors develop, and how they may be changed. You will learn how to use tools that work for the majority of those who employ them. *Powerless No Longer* will teach you that you have everything you need to recover. The rest is up to you.

A glance at what works

What works? There is no easy and simple answer. No program, drug, or method works for everyone under all circumstances. There are commonalities among the methods used by study subjects who quit on their own, and that's where we will focus our attention.

We will draw common threads from the studies of the effectiveness of the methods used by the various programs and treatment centers. There will be surprises for those with preconceived notions, but the bottom line is that the most successful approaches involve a combination of methods. We shall go wherever the data leads us.

The element most common to successful recoveries achieved by any method is finding the resolve or motivation necessary to make a major life change. This is true no matter what the addiction, or the relative severity. If motivated, almost anything will work; in the absence of motivation, nothing will. The necessary catalyst may come from any source; the most common is a single consultation with a trusted medical professional, like a family doctor. Other important sources of motivation are family or financial pressures, a major life event, or a "moment of clarity."

Substantial lifestyle change is the second commonality.

Such things as ending associations with using friends, finding substitute activities, and discovering ways to cope with the urges and cravings that drive many of us back into addictive behavior. Studies show that the majority who succeed used a support network of friends and family members.

Learning how to get along on a daily basis without resorting to the drugs we were using to kill pain and alter reality is another common thread. Most of us have learned to see the world differently than our non-using friends. We are more susceptible to stress than most, and our belief systems must undergo a major change in order for us to obtain long-term sobriety. To modify our belief systems, we change the way we think about our relationships and even ourselves. This requires directed effort; it does not happen by itself.

Many of us who started using at a young age never "grew up." We didn't learn the value of working for the achievement of long-term goals. We were much more into short-term gratification, and a life spent in the pursuit of the pleasures of the moment, centered upon using. As my drinking increased, my world shrank, and alcohol took away the things I enjoyed. Woodworking went first, followed by reading, sports, clubs, and finally I withdrew from my family and most of the outside world. It amazes me even today that I accepted this as normal, and even desirable. When I quit, I discovered there *is* a life out there, and I could be part of it without drinking! My goodness, there *is* life after alcohol, who knew?

Every successful recovering person goes through this process. We learn to restore balance in our lives, to manage short and long-term goals, and interact with other people on an equal footing. We accept personal responsibility for our actions, which we seldom did when we were using. These are learned skills, and whether we get them from a program, from friends and family, or from a professional, we need them for long-term success in our new lives.

Underlying all of the above is an ancient technique called *mindfulness meditation,* a tool used to focus our attention upon the present moment. We act as we feel, and we feel as we think, so our thoughts drive our behavior. The above suggestions for change share the common purpose of altering our thinking, our beliefs, and subsequently our behavior. Our goal is to change our thoughts and feelings, and the practice of mindfulness provides a reliable method of monitoring them on an ongoing basis. That's the object of mindfulness meditation.

A final word before we begin

After the incident with my daughter, I didn't put a gun to my head, nor did I continue to drink beyond the next day. Instead, I found door number three. I discovered there is a way to live that doesn't require constant alteration of reality. *Powerless No Longer* is the story of how I discovered that life, and how most addicts discover it either on their own, or with minimal help.

. This effort grew out of curiosity that began when I was attending Alcoholics Anonymous meetings, but didn't buy the "higher power" concept or believe that I was powerless. I never worked a step, used a sponsor, prayed, or followed most of the other "suggestions," except for one: I didn't drink. Why was I successful when studies show that only five out of every one hundred people stay sober for a year in AA?[1] I drifted away after a few years, never to return.

When Mike Werner, one of the founders of SMART

Recovery®, introduced me to their scientifically based program, I learned most addicts recover on their own, or with minimal help. Mike and I started a SMART meeting that's still going strong in Wilmington, North Carolina. As I was learning how addicts recover, I became curious about how addiction works, why I behaved as I did, and why I continued to drink even when I received little benefit from the drug. I did the research necessary to learn the answers to these questions, and many more, discovering that the principles governing the conventional recovery establishment have little or no relevance to how addiction works, or how addicts recover.

Powerless No Longer is for anyone who is concerned about an addictive behavior problem and is looking for help deciding upon a course of action. The book introduces a newcomer to the science of addiction, the process of change, and specific methods and tools that offer a way out. The rest will be up to you.

If you want your life to continue the way it is, close the book now, put it down and step away—or offer it to a friend. One thing is for certain; don't expect this book, or any book, to cure your addiction without a *great deal* of effort on your part. The same goes for any of the programs, methods, techniques, or available drugs. There is no silver bullet!

You *do* need to tap into a source of power and strength, but it isn't outside, it's internal. If you possess a genuine desire to effect self-change in any area of your life, you have within yourself all the power you need.

Chapter 2: Natural Recovery

What is natural recovery?

Natural recovery is the spontaneous remission of addictive behavior without professional treatment, or use of self-help groups. Many specialists in the treatment field are skeptical of the notion that addicts can recover without professional help, as is the public. The idea of self-managed recovery contradicts the concept of addiction as a disease that is, in principle, irreversible and progressive. The studies in this chapter show that a high percentage of addicts self-remit with little or no outside help. For most of these studies, attendance at a few self-help meetings, as long as the addict does not enter formal treatment, is considered natural recovery.

The American Psychiatric Association (APA) publishes a book called *the Diagnostic and Statistical Manual of Mental Disorders*, commonly called the DSM. By the time I publish this book, the current version will be the DSM-V. Professionals in the field use the DSM to diagnose behavioral-health problems. There has been controversy over the changes in the new version of the DSM, but they are not important for our purposes.

The following studies referenced the criteria that existed in the DSM-IV. The two categories of substance use disorders are abuse and dependence, with abuse being the milder disorder. Below are the criteria from the DSM-IV.

Substance Abuse: one or more of the following within a 12-month period:

1. *Recurrent substance use resulting in a failure to fulfill major role obligations at work, school, or home (such as repeated absences or poor work performance related to substance use; substance-related absences, suspensions, or expulsions from school; or neglect of children or household).*

2. *Recurrent substance use in situations in which it is physically hazardous (such as driving an automobile or operating a machine when impaired by substance use).*

3. *Recurrent substance-related legal problems (such as arrests for substance related disorderly conduct).*

4. *Continued substance use despite having persistent or recurrent social or interpersonal problems caused or exacerbated by the effects of the substance (for example, arguments with spouse about consequences of intoxication and physical fights).*

Substance Dependence: three (or more) of the following occurring anytime in the same 12-month period:

1. *Tolerance, as defined by either of the following: (a) a need for markedly increased amounts of the substance to achieve intoxication or the desired effect or (b) markedly diminished effect with continued use of the same amount of substance.*

2. *Withdrawal, as manifested by either of the*

following: (a) the characteristic withdrawal syndrome for the substance or (b) the same (or closely related) substance is taken to relieve or avoid withdrawal symptoms.

3. *The substance is often taken in larger amounts or over a longer period then intended.*

4. *There is a persistent desire or unsuccessful efforts to cut down or control substance use.*

5. *A great deal of time is spent in activities necessary to obtain the substance, use the substance, or recover from its effects.*

6. *Important social, occupational, or recreational activities are given up or reduced because of substance use.*

The substance use is continued despite knowledge of having a persistent physical or psychological problem that is likely to have been caused or exacerbated by the substance (for example, current cocaine use despite recognition of cocaine-induced depression or continued drinking despite recognition that an ulcer was made worse by alcohol consumption.[2]

The new version of the DSM eliminates the "abuse" and "dependence" categories, and replaces them with a new category: "Addictions and related disorders," retaining the same criteria. There is one added criteria in the new DSM: craving, which they define as a "strong desire or urge to use a specific substance." Otherwise, the criteria are the same as, except for the rating system, moderate or severe, with or without tolerance or withdrawal.

I hope I did not confuse you with these different versions of the DSM. I wanted to include the criteria because the studies refer to them, and the criteria provide a benchmark to help us define addiction.

Natural recovery from nicotine

How many people do you know who have quit smoking without using formal programs, self-help groups, or nicotine replacement therapy (NRT)? The American Heart Association says that nicotine is one of the most addictive substances, weaving itself into virtually every facet of a smoker's life. From an article by The National Institute on Drug Abuse:

> *"Research has shown how nicotine acts on the brain to produce a number of effects. Of primary importance to its addictive nature are findings that nicotine activates reward pathways—the brain circuitry that regulates feelings of pleasure...nicotine increases levels of dopamine in the reward circuits. This reaction is similar to that seen with other drugs of abuse... For many tobacco users, long-term brain changes induced by continued nicotine exposure result in addiction."*[3]

Therefore, nicotine works the same way, and to the same extent as other drugs of abuse. Anyone who has ever tried to quit smoking understands how addictive it can be.

I tried to quit smoking many times over the years, using every method or program available, but nothing worked. Patches, pills, gum, hypnosis, acupuncture, I tried everything. What finally worked for me was a ten-minute talk with my cardiologist as she was releasing me from the hospital after I suffered a major heart attack in 1999. I quit cold turkey. Of course, I had been in intensive care for a week, and they frown upon smoking there, so I had a head start. Still, I had strong urges off and on for weeks, and I must say that quitting smoking was much harder than quitting drinking.

In 1986, the American Cancer Society reported that *"over 90% of the estimated 37,000,000 people who have stopped smoking in this country since the Surgeon General's first report linking smoking to cancer have done so unaided."* [4]

An article in the August 2007 edition of the *American Journal of Public Health* said that over 75% of those who quit for 7 to 24 months did so without any help, as opposed to 12.5% who used NRT (patch or gum).[5] A study in the February 2008 issue of the *American Journal of Preventive Medicine* indicated that almost 65% of quitters used no help, while around 30% used medication, and 9% used behavioral treatment.[6]

The following appeared in *PLoS Medicine*, an open access, peer-reviewed medical journal in February of 2010:

> *"As with problem drinking, gambling, and narcotics use, population studies show consistently that a large majority of smokers who permanently stop smoking do so without any form of assistance... [T]he most common method used by most people who have successfully stopped smoking remains unassisted cessation... Up to three-quarters of ex-smokers have quit without assistance ('cold turkey' or cut down then quit) and unaided cessation is by far the most common method used by most successful ex-smokers."* [7]

The evidence shows that unassisted quit attempts have a much greater chance of success than those using NRT's, hypnosis, or any other method. The pharmaceutical industry continues to fund advertising campaigns to convince the public and physicians that quitting "cold turkey," without help, is a waste of time, and doomed to failure.

Because most assisted quit attempts end in relapse, smokers could interpret the failure risks as 'I tried and failed using a method that my doctor said had the best success rate. Trying to quit unaided—which I never hear recommended— would be a waste of time.' One review stated "...*such reasoning might well disempower smokers and inhibit quit attempts through anticipatory, self-defeating fatalism.*" [8] In other words, if the pills and patches do not work for them, they will probably just give up.

The evidence shows that empowering people with the belief they can quit smoking on their own is much more effective than feeding them the nonsense that they are powerless.

Early studies of self-change

There were no studies of self-remitters before the 1960s and 70s. The main reason was that by the early 1960's, the "disease model" had become the foundation of addiction research and policy in the United States. According to that model addiction is irreversible, always progressive, and once addicted the addict is powerless over his disease and cannot recover without help. In addition, according to the model, narcotic drugs (opium and derivatives) had properties that enslaved even casual users, instantly and for life.

Instead of studies, resources went into treatment centers

for alcoholics, based upon the 12-step model, and the prevention of any use of narcotic drugs. The suggestion that alcohol dependence or heroin use might be temporary conditions that the afflicted might address on their own, struck at the heart of widespread and firmly rooted beliefs, challenging strong and powerful vested interests in the prevention and treatment fields.

Another major reason there were no studies was that the phenomenon of self-remission was largely unknown because of the population the researchers were seeing. The only addicts the researchers saw were those whose problems were severe enough to come to the attention of society, those who wound up behind bars or in treatment centers. The vast majority of drug and alcohol abusers who were addressing their problems on their own without help were invisible.

A researcher named Charles Winick noticed that two-thirds of the 16,000 addicts who were reported as regular users to the Federal Bureau of Narcotics between 1953 and 1954 were not reported again at the end of 1959. He concluded that, allowing for a number who died, the rest had ceased their drug use. He also found that three-quarters of the over 7,000 addicts who had quit between 1955 and 1960 had stopped their drug use before age 38. In addition, more than 80% stopped using before the tenth year of their addiction.

The conclusion Winick drew was that there might be a natural life cycle of heroin addiction. After learning to cope with the stresses that drove them to drugs in the first place, addicts were able to "mature out" of their addictions.[9]

In 1968, an Australian psychiatrist Les Drew noticed that many clinical studies showed the number of alcoholics in relation to the population peaked before the age of 50, and then declined. Although he felt some of the decline was due to the increased mortality rate among alcoholics, he did not believe that factor alone was enough to account for the differences he saw, nor were the effects of treatment programs. He began to believe that a self-change process might account for a significant number of the alcoholics who disappear from alcohol statistics as they get older. He believed that the factors that might accompany aging, and account for the statistics were things like increasing maturity, responsibility, and family and social pressures.[10]

What made his paper (along with Winick's) something of a ground breaker was that together, they made a strong case that substance dependence was not always a progressive and irreversible condition, the widely-accepted belief at the time. It took years for researchers and treatment professionals to recognize the tremendous difference in the appearance of addiction between the general population and those who ended up in treatment.

The Vietnam veterans study

Opiates and other drugs were easily available in Vietnam, and large numbers of service personnel appeared to be using them on a regular basis. The Nixon administration set up a series of studies to estimate the size of the drug use problem, and plan for proper treatment facilities for returning addicted veterans. The studies looked at two samples of enlisted men who left Vietnam to return home in September of 1971. They chose one sample on a random basis from all returnees and the other from those who had screened "drug positive" before departure.

The studies found that almost half of all enlisted men

had used narcotics while in Vietnam, 34% had tried heroin, and 38% had tried opium. Almost half of those who had used narcotics had done so more than weekly for greater than 6 months. Overall, 20% of all returning men admitted to having been "addicted" to narcotics while in Vietnam. That is, they had felt "strung out," and experienced repeated and prolonged withdrawal symptoms.

During the first year after return, about 10% of the general sample and one-third of those who had tested "positive" at departure proved to have used any narcotics. Less than 1 in 10 of all men who had used since returning had experienced any signs of addiction. Only 7% in the drug-positive sample and 12% of all men who had been addicted in Vietnam were still addicted after returning.[11]

Following the veterans for another two years, fewer than 20% of those who were addicted in Vietnam had resumed regular narcotic use for three years after return. Only 2% of those who had used narcotics in Vietnam, and 6% of those in the "drug-positive" sample ever attended drug-abuse treatment, therefore treatment had little to do with the remarkable recovery rates.[12]

A 25-year follow-up conducted with the remaining members of the original study group produced the following results:

A. most attempted to quit and the majority succeeded at the time of their last try without the aid of traditional drug treatment programs

B. less than 9% of current drug users had been treated in a formal treatment setting

C. *"Most drug abusers who had started using drugs by their*

early 20s appeared to gradually achieve remission.
Spontaneous remission was the rule rather than the
exception. "[13]

The overwhelming majority of heroin users who returned from Vietnam with a problem solved it by themselves, without treatment facilities or self-help programs. They found the power within themselves, and quit on their own.

The end of the powerless myth

Two researchers, Hasin and Grant, carried out the first large-scale study of natural recovery in 1995. This large study used a sample of 44,000 people in all 50 states and the District of Columbia. They identified former drinkers, 19% of the total sample, or more than 8,000 people. Of these, 21% were alcohol dependent and 42% were alcohol abusers according to DSM-IV criteria. Only 33% of the dependent people and 17% who were alcohol abusers had attended AA, or sought any other type of treatment.

Out of over 8,000 former drinkers, 3,500 were alcohol abusers, and 1,700 met the criteria for alcohol dependence. Of the abusers, 83% quit on their own, along with 67% of those dependent upon alcohol. Overall, in this important study, 77% of those diagnosed with alcohol abuse or dependence quit on their own, without treatment, AA, or help of any kind.[14]

There are several large Canadian studies of recovery without treatment. Using data from a national survey of nearly 12,000, and an Ontario survey of over 1,000, a study of those who self-remitted found recovery rates about the same as the American study mentioned above. 77.6% of those who quit did so on their own without help of any kind.[15]

Another American study, the National Epidemiologic Survey on Alcohol and Related Conditions (NESARC), in 2005, involved a sample size of over 43,000 adults. The study classified 4,500 people with DSM-IV substance dependence. Only 25.6% of the sample had ever sought help for their dependence. The study showed that of those who remitted in the last year, 72.4% did so without formal help.[16]

Another natural recovery study involved several groups of dependent drinkers. One group had serious alcohol problems over many years and resolved them through abstinence or treatment, while another group experienced fewer problems but "matured out" of them as they aged. Yet another group recovered, and was able to drink with fewer problems than the abstinent groups. In this study, self-recoveries varied between 53.7% and 87.5% depending upon the number of DSM-IV problems the drinker had experienced. Even among those who had six or more problems, however, 53.7% recovered without formal treatment. As with the other studies, recoveries with and without treatment were lower as the number of DSM-IV problems increased.[17]

A study of older, untreated alcoholics involved 2,000 individuals recruited from a larger community sample. Data from four and 10-year follow-ups showed that 73% of these 51 to 65-year-olds remitted without any formal help.[18]

These are just a very few of the several hundred studies that have looked at untreated remission of drug and alcohol abuse and dependence over the past forty years. Taken overall, the studies indicate that self-change accounts for three-quarters of all successful recoveries from substance abuse and dependency problems.

Successful non-abstinent outcomes

Many of the studies and reviews undertaken in the last several years have shown low-risk alcohol use among former abusers and dependents as a widespread and frequent occurrence. In a review of 28 natural recovery studies undertaken in 2000, 22 of the 28 studies (78%) showed significant levels of low-risk drinking on the part of the participants. As many as one-third were able to return to moderate drinking, to the point where they no longer met DSM-IV criteria.[19] In the same review of 15 additional studies, 13 of the 15 (86.6%) showed the same results. A similar pattern emerged among drug users, where nearly half the studies reported limited drug use recoveries.[20]

These results are the same as those from several alcohol treatment outcome studies, which capture degree of abstinence over time, and together these data suggest that viewing abstinence as the only possible outcome for all drug and alcohol abusers is neither practical nor realistic.[21], [22]

Conclusion

The disease model of addiction, that has dominated the treatment field for decades, implies that you are powerless over your addiction, and therefore cannot find any meaningful recovery on your own. I hope that the examples and studies I have presented in this chapter have at least begun to convince you otherwise. If nothing else, you now know what researchers in the field have known for many years: that most addicts recover without formal help, and so can you.

Chapter 3: Learning Addiction

Growing and changing

Most recovery books explain the mechanism of addiction by discussing the chemical changes that take place in the brain during the various phases of the addiction process. I am not denying that these chemical changes happen, just that they do not affect our ability to overcome our addictions by changing our thoughts, beliefs, and actions. There's another way to explain the development of addiction that is equally valid and does a better job of explaining how we become dependent upon substances, and how we recover.

Our brains have the ability to rewire themselves, changing structurally and functionally, in response to changes in our environment and our day-to-day experiences. New evidence, including detailed fMRI imaging, shows that our brains keep the ability to change into adulthood and even old age. Our experiences can alter the brain's physical structure and functional organization from top to bottom.[23]

This characteristic of the brain, called *neuroplasticity*, is responsible for our learning and unlearning, and for the ability of some people to recover from serious injuries, strokes, and diseases that disable or disrupt their brain functions.

Why am I taking this route when most other books on addiction discuss the chemistry that drives the changes? I do it for two important reasons:

1. Understanding that we *learn* to become addicted is

an important key to overcoming it, and the underlying chemistry that drives addiction learning doesn't matter. In fact, the chemistry varies from drug to drug, while the learning process remains the same.

2. We do not recover from addiction chemically. We recover by changing our thoughts, feelings, beliefs, and therefore our actions.

Recovery is an unlearning *and* a learning process, which, in the context of neuroplasticity, works in the same manner as addiction itself, making the whole procedure much easier to explain.

To draw a sports analogy, if you were teaching your child to hit a baseball, would you tell them to contract this muscle or that, when, and to what degree for a hundred different muscles? Of course you wouldn't. You would just tell them to keep their eye on the ball, their shoulders level, take a good swing, and follow-through. As we go through this discussion, I believe you will understand why I chose to do it this way.

At birth, our brains contained approximately 100,000,000,000 (one hundred *billion)* nerve cells, called neurons. Each neuron has the ability to connect to as many as 100,000 other neurons. The *synapse* is the point of connection between them, a gap, a millionth of a centimeter wide. Through these tiny gaps flow our thoughts, emotions, and sensory perceptions. Around age three, the average neuron makes 15,000 connections with other neurons. In the adult brain, the total number of connections, or synapses, can be as many as one thousand *trillion!*[24]

Our genes dictate some of the connections we are born

with. The human genome has 35,000 operative genes, and just half of those are involved in the brain. Most of the connections that are active in our brains right now are the result of our environment and experiences, not heredity.

We eliminate unused synapses. By one estimate, we lose twenty *billion* a day between childhood and early adolescence. Connections we do not use wither and die, while at the same time we are continually forming new connections as we learn about the world around us and interact with others.[25]

One more concept is necessary to understand neuroplasticity, and that's the issue of *synaptic strength*. When two connected neurons are both active a good deal of the time, the synapse changes in a way that makes the activation of one cell more likely to cause the other cell to fire.[26] This is the maxim "cells that fire together, wire together." Picture a well used dirt road in the country, with deep ruts worn by generations of traffic, making it easy to stay on the path. Or schoolchildren learning the multiplication tables, repeating them over and over, until constant use allows them to remember that seven times seven is forty-nine without having to do any conscious computation. That is the concept of synaptic strength.

To communicate with one another, neurons synthesize chemicals called *neurotransmitters,* which flow from one side of the synaptic gap and attach to receptors on the other side. They perform the dual role of transmitting signals and modulating signals already there. Information flows through the neuron because of a difference in electrical potential. This difference in potential produces an electrical current, and when it reaches a sufficient level, it forces a release of neurotransmitters from one neuron to the other.

We forge long-term memories, and learn new habits and skills by strengthening neural connections through repetition, trauma, reward, or mindfulness. Events like Pearl Harbor, the Kennedy assassination, and the horror of 9/11 can imprint permanent memories by their magnitude, and their effects upon our lives and our emotions. Any of us who lived through them remember where we were and what we were doing when we first heard about them. Few of us could recall what we did on the preceding day. We are all familiar with that sort of memory imprinting and recall, but what about the normal, everyday things we try to remember. How does neuroplasticity work?

Neuroplasticity is the selective organizing of connections of neurons in our brains. When we practice an activity or access a memory we have already formed, our neural networks—groups of neurons that fire together, shape themselves according to that activity or memory. When we stop practicing these things, our brains will eliminate or "prune" the connecting cells that formed the pathways. As in a system of freeways connecting various cities, the more cars going to a certain destination, the wider the road that carries them needs to be. Fewer cars, fewer lanes are needed.

Learning through experience

The first step in memory formation, called "encoding," is a biological process rooted in the senses that begins with perception. As an example, think of meeting your first "crush." When you met him or her, your visual system registered things like their physical appearance, the color of their eyes, the tilt of their head, and their smile. Your auditory system may have recorded the sound of their laughter.

Perhaps you experienced the smell of their after-shave or perfume. You may have even felt the touch of their hand upon your arm. These separate sensations traveled along neural pathways from different regions to a part of your brain stem called the *hippocampus*. Here they integrate, and become one single experience—your experience of that specific person. [27]

Imaging studies show that the hippocampus, along with another part of our brain, called the *frontal cortex* analyzes these various sensory inputs and decides if they're worth remembering or not. If they are, they become part of our long-term memory. If not, they stay briefly in short-term memory before they are lost. Short-term memory is analogous to RAM memory in a computer. As I am writing this on my computer, the words I type, and the changes I make are stored temporarily in RAM. When I click the "save" button, my changes are written to the computer's hard drive, the equivalent of long-term memory. If the computer loses power while I am typing, or I forget to save my changes to the hard drive, they are lost forever.

Do we have any control over what information we retain in our long-term memory? Yes we do. There are tools we can use to train our minds to commit information to long-term memory, on our internal hard drives. One tool is repetition, and the other is mindfulness.

If we perform a task or recall information that causes groups of connected neurons to fire in concert, it strengthens the connections between those cells, and they become what we call *declarative memory*. This is the long-term memory we use in conscious decision-making. If we strengthen them enough, these pathways become what we call *working or habit memory*, and we can recall information, or perform tasks *without the intervention or collaboration of our conscious mind!* Practice makes permanent. The more times the network is stimulated, the stronger and more efficient it becomes.

There is nothing harder in sports than to hit a good major-league pitcher, but a great hitter never thinks about all the muscles that have to move in perfect coordination to hit the ball. He makes a decision in a few milliseconds, and well-developed neural pathways do the rest. A concert pianist does not consciously control his fingers while playing a piece he has practiced his whole life. We do not think about the answer to seven-times-seven, or our own social security number. These things have been committed to what we call "working" or "habit" memory. We do not think about riding a bike, or turning on the tap when we are thirsty, we just do it. If you have ever found yourself staring into an open refrigerator without knowing how you got there, you have experienced habit memory.

Many recent studies have shown that mindfulness can play a major role in the retention of information. [28] By mindfulness in this context, I am referring to just paying attention, or being in the moment and present to our lives. How many times have you been reading and "read" several pages and cannot remember even one of them because your mind drifted off? Alternatively, you are having a conversation with a friend, and suddenly discover that you cannot recall a single word they have said for the last minute or two?

We can focus for a time, but without some mindfulness training, it is difficult for us to keep ourselves from wandering off on a mental adventure. Paying attention is one of the best ways to improve our chances of retaining information, and making major changes in the way we think, and perceive the world around us. If you want to increase your chances of remembering where you left your car keys last night, be sure you are "present" when you set them down.

Learning through reward

Headquartered in a part of our brain that evolved hundreds of millions of years ago, is the system that incentivizes us to eat, reproduce, defend ourselves, protect our young, and perform other important functions that are key to our survival and the survival of our species. Called the *reward pathway*, or *limbic system*, it is one of the most powerful and complex systems we have.

Sometimes referred to as our "reptile brain," because of its early evolution, this system organizes the behaviors that are life-sustaining, provides the tools necessary to take the desired actions, and then rewards us with pleasure when we do. Research shows that almost any activity we find pleasurable, from eating a chocolate chip cookie to hearing great music or seeing a beautiful face, can activate the reward system. Once aroused, these circuits enable our brains to encode the circumstances that led to the pleasure, so that we can repeat the behavior and the reward in the future.

A critical part of this system is a chemical called dopamine. Released from neurons in the reward system circuits, it functions as a neurotransmitter, heightening our awareness and focusing our attention. Many other sections of the brain are part of this network, including decision-making areas like the frontal cortex. The neural pathways in this system are the most-used and strongest pathways in our entire brain. There is no other system, no other stimulus that will drive the formation of new connections or the strengthening of existing ones faster than the reward, or limbic system. [29] This system connects the higher and lower functions of our brains and serves as its emotional center.

When we experience a positive, pleasurable outcome from an action or event, the release of dopamine alters the brain circuitry, providing tools and encouragement to repeat the event. The memory circuitry stores cues, or triggers, to the rewarding stimulus. Previously neutral cues (a perfume, a particular location) now become important. Our brains map the environment in which we experience the rewarding activity by recording the place, the people, the smells, and the entire incident. Triggers alone are not enough; actions are necessary to get a reward. The system engages the areas of the brain that control our ability to take action. [30]

When we experience a rewarding event, the thinking portions of our brain engage. We remember the actions used to achieve the reward and create the capacity to repeat the experience. Not only does a pleasurable experience result in pleasant memories, the executive center of the brain provides motivation, rationalization, and the activation of other brain areas necessary to repeat the experience. Each time we repeat the experience, these changes and reorganizations become stronger and more ingrained.

The memory formation process is the same for reward-driven memories as for stimulus-driven. The key difference between the two is that following the initial encoding or acquisition phase, the stronger emotions and already well-established neural pathways involved with the reward structure leads to much more rapid formation of declarative and working or habit memory. As we will see next, the reward system is the one hijacked by addiction.

From Reward to Slavery

The word "addiction" is from a Latin term meaning, "enslaved by" or "bound to." Anyone who has struggled to overcome an addiction—or has tried to help someone else to do so—understands why. Addiction is a continuum. There are degrees of severity; it is not an on-or-off condition. In Chapter 2, we saw that the criteria become more severe as the disorder progresses. In this section, we are going to look at addiction from a new direction—that of neuroplasticity. If a large part of addiction is learned behavior, how and why does it happen? How can we reverse or countermand the learned part of the process?

Earlier, we learned the three phases, or stages of normal learning. The acquisition phase, where we gather sensory data and decide what to do with it; the declarative phase, or memory we use in conscious decision-making; and working or habit memory, which governs actions we take without the intervention or collaboration of our conscious mind. Although behavioral characteristics vary with the particular drug, there are three distinct stages in the process of addiction, which correspond to the three memory phases. [31]

All drugs of abuse trigger the limbic system by stimulating the release of dopamine in the neurons.[32], [33] This stimulation focuses our attention, gives us pleasure, and causes our brain circuitry to record the entire experience, so we can repeat it in the future. Because it is the limbic system, the message is powerful, and even the early experiences encode strongly.[34] The dopamine release triggered by drug use is two to ten times stronger and of much longer duration than that of normal biological rewards.[35] For those rewards, (eating, sex, etc.) once we learn the most efficient behavior to obtain a reward, further dopamine release is not necessary and does not occur.[36] Sufficient drug use, however, always produces a dopamine release, even in chronic users.[37]

During this initial phase, which corresponds to the acquisition stage of memory development, we store cues, triggers, and everything relevant about the experiences we are having. To a non-smoker, the ringing of a telephone, a cup of coffee, or ordering a drink, are not triggers that bring a cigarette to mind. They were to me when I was a smoker. Lines of white powder on a tabletop, a syringe, or the sight of a crack pipe, are not triggers or cues for me. I did not use those particular drugs, so I have no memories associated with the drugs themselves, the acts necessary to use them, or the environment in which they are used. However, a friendly pub, a glass of scotch, or the sight of a cold beer on a hot day, would have been a different story for me, thirty years ago.

While we are socially using, we receive positive feedback from the drug. The world seems brighter, and many of us believe we fit in better than before. We are more comfortable with ourselves, and others. We notice that the drug mitigates many of the everyday stressors we face—at least for a while. As long as the experience remains pleasant overall, we tend to repeat it, putting up with occasional hangovers, bad experiences, and minor negative occurrences. In the meantime, we are learning that drug-seeking behavior is more important than seeking normal rewards—like sex or a good meal. Each time a drug is used, the pathways that record the surrounding events get stronger and more ingrained.

The limbic system did not evolve to addict us to cocaine or alcohol; it evolved to provide a powerful incentive to survive and reproduce. After we learn a pleasurable behavior, sex, for instance, certain cues will cause a release of dopamine when there appears to be any chance of the pleasurable activity occurring. A glimpse of an attractive person at a cocktail party, for instance, can trigger the limbic system. Your pulse quickens, your attention focuses, and your brain engages. It is no different with addiction. Once the patterns are well established, the slightest cue or trigger is enough to release dopamine and begin drug-seeking behavior. [38]

The second stage of addiction, referred to as *regulated relapse,* corresponds to the use of declarative memory in conscious decision-making. A cue or trigger activates the reward system, and first we consider if using is appropriate. If it is we do it, if not, we put it off. If we choose not to use, the chance of impending reward disappears, so dopamine levels will slowly return to normal, until the next cue or trigger. There is no rule governing the beginning (or for that matter the end) of this stage. It varies from person to person and from drug to drug.

One defining characteristic of regulated relapse is tolerance—it takes more of the drug to achieve the same effects. The brain reacts to repeated drug exposure by changing itself physically and chemically to offset the effect of the drug. If the drug causes the release of large amounts of a particular neurotransmitter, for instance, the brain will decrease the number of receptors for that neurotransmitter. Thereafter, larger amounts of the drug are necessary to achieve the same effects. Withdrawing the drug leaves the brain unbalanced because it is now dependent upon the drug. [39]

If the pattern reoccurs often enough for long enough, the addict moves on to the third stage of addiction, called *compulsive relapse.* This corresponds to the formation of working or habit memory. There is little conscious thought involved in the decision to use because it is very difficult for the executive decision-making capacity to intrude upon the drug-seeking behavior.[40] fMRI imaging of addicts presented with various using cues shows very little involvement of areas of the brain used in decision-making.[41]

There is an additional force that drives compulsive using in this stage—negative reinforcement, or the "gotta have its." If we do not eat for a long time, our limbic system makes us feel uncomfortable, causes that pain in the belly, and focuses our attention on obtaining that next meal. The longer we go without eating, the higher our anxiety level, and the more focused we become. The urge to use becomes exactly like that—an overwhelming force screaming that it has to have the drug, that using is a life-and-death situation the addict cannot ignore. With most drugs, there are also withdrawal symptoms that help drive us to use. At this point, the addict puts the drug ahead of everything: spouse, family, job, and goals. Nothing will interfere with the overwhelming need for the drug. The addict will continue to use in spite of severe negative consequences.

The journey to addiction begins with our receiving positive reinforcement from use of the drug—it makes us feel good, and ends with the "gotta have its" screaming in our ear. For some, it seems like a hopeless situation, but the vast majority of us find a solution to the problem, and so can you.

Replacing learned behaviors

Up to now, we have been discussing neuroplasticity as though our brain is a one-way street, but that is not the case.

Our brain is fluid; we can replace old knowledge, ideas, beliefs, and habits with new ones. Pathways we do not use shrivel up and die. We forget people, places, and things. We lose skills acquired with a great deal of effort. We change habits, likes, dislikes, political parties; we adapt new ways of doing things, discarding the old. In other words, if we are the sum of our experiences, we become different people over time, and this results from neuroplasticity.

Baseball players have batting practice every day. Actors rehearse again, and again, and again. We must practice every skill we learn, to keep the neural circuits we have created, or we lose them. Jascha Heifetz, the renowned violinist said: "If I don't practice one day, *I* know it; two days, the *critics* know it; three days, the *public* knows it."

Neglect and atrophy are not the only way our circuits can change. When we change our minds about something, we *really change our minds*. When we receive new information that changes how we think or feel about someone or something, we alter synaptic connections all over our brains. Neurons that used to be connected to one place are now connected somewhere else, firing with different neural circuits. [42] We do not have to worry about the mechanics of it, we just make a decision, and neuroplasticity does it.

Just as new information that we deem important can change our thinking and our beliefs, we can also change habit or working memory using the same tools. Let's say we have always done something a certain way, perhaps because a parent or teacher showed us early in life, and now we find a new way to do it that's more efficient and produces a better result. It might be a woodworking technique, a golf swing, or a sewing method; what it is does not matter. We can change habitual behavior. All that's required is that we pay attention, and practice the new method or behavior until it becomes our new habit. Connections that existed will disappear, replaced by the new connections we create.

Change is not easy, and I do not mean to leave you with the impression that it is. What I am saying is that your brain is constantly changing, and *you* have ultimate control over it—for good or ill. Just because your brain forms certain connections and you have learned to respond to certain cues and triggers in particular ways, does not mean you cannot make new connections, and form new habits that override and supersede the old. In the next chapter, we will map the process of change, for the more we understand it, the less we fear it.

Chapter 4: Taking the Fear Out of Change

Fear keeps us in place

Change can be frightening. The greater the modification we are attempting, the more we fear it. If you are still with me, you are at least contemplating making a major change in your life. Trying to substitute one behavior for another, one belief system for another can lead to the kind of fear that paralyzes us to the point where we are too frightened to move ahead. I think most of us have experienced that fear, and sometimes it intimidates us into making a decision to stay where we are, rather than trying to change our behavior.

In the beginning of the first chapter, I described how I felt before I passed out the night before I quit drinking. I had no idea what the next day was going to bring. I reached the point where I couldn't continue to drink, and yet I didn't know how to stop, or even if I could survive without alcohol to kill the pain. I had two survival instincts fighting one another, both telling me I was going to die if I chose the wrong path.

Some addicts reach that point and are not motivated enough to take the plunge and quit, preferring the devil they know to the devil they don't. My purpose here is to shine a light on the change process itself, to remove the mystery and some of the fear along with it.

A simple model of change

There are as many paths to recovery as people who are successful. Regardless of the path we choose, we all go through the same stages. This chapter is about what these stages of change are, what triggers them, how you tell what stage you are in, and how you begin. This is the *process* of change, as we learned it from the millions of people who overcame not only substance dependency, but also many other problems.

In a 1984 paper, two researchers, James Prochaska and Carlo DiClemente, proposed a five-stage model of change (later expanded to six stages) to explain the theories of therapy being used in smoking cessation. Their *Transtheoretical Model of Behavior Change* (TTM) has become an accepted standard for representing the process of change in many different areas of behavior, including addiction.

To their six-stage model, I chose to add one more— relapse, which is included in many programs that use the TTM to illustrate change. Approximately 43% of self-remitters recover on their first try, leaving 57% who relapse at least once, making relapse a normal part of the process and certainly worth talking about.

The stages are:

- **Precontemplation:** Not considering change because they do not see the need.

- **Contemplation:** Considering change, and beginning to see the connection between the problems in their lives and the substances they are using.

- **Preparation:** Making plans to change, and deciding upon the method.

- **Action:** Taking the actions necessary to bring about change.

- **Maintenance:** Doing what is necessary to maintain the changes they have made.

- **Relapse:** An optional stage, more of an event, and not a requirement for recovery.

- **Termination:** After a process of change, thoughts, beliefs, and actions are no longer the same; these are ex-users moving on with their lives.

Many researchers consider behavior change a much more complex issue than these stages describe, and others maintain that many people change without going through all of the stages. For example, many of the substance abusers who recovered on their own in the studies presented in the second chapter completed the change as soon as they decided to stop. What we can learn from this is that change, like substance abuse itself, is a continuum.

I will be using the transtheoretical model to illustrate the change process because it offers a way to bring order to a very complex situation. I will cover each of the stages, with emphasis upon what is necessary to move to the next stage. Three things you might like to keep in mind:

1. There is no time limit because we are all individuals, and we change at different rates.

2. Moving between stages is what causes the most pain and requires the most effort.

3. Change is a continuum, and sometimes it is difficult to tell what stage you are in.

The precontemplative – living in denial

Most of us go on with our destructive habits for years

until something awakens us. It is impossible to predict what it will take to make an individual aware of their condition. Early in my own recovery, I accompanied some AA friends to a minimum-security prison for alcohol-related automobile offenses in Connecticut. These inmates all had repeated arrests for DUI and some were serving time for killing or injuring innocent people while driving under the influence.

I talked with these fellows, and to a man, they just couldn't wait to get back out and "have a beer." They were locked up, separated from friends and family, in deep legal trouble, and couldn't connect the troubles they were in to the alcohol. In their minds, the problem wasn't the substance; it was always something "else," something totally out of their control that was responsible for their current situation.

It may sound as though I'm judging those inmates; believe me, nothing is further from the truth. I had tons of evidence over many years that my drinking was out of control and chose not to make the connection or do anything about it. I believed what I was doing was normal and a natural reaction to the way the rest of the world was treating me. There is also the normal human tendency to discount evidence, even very strong evidence, which contradicts something we already believe. The more deeply held the belief, the stronger the evidence needed to falsify the belief.

In this stage, addicts have not made a decision to change. They are either unaware their using is causing a problem in their life, or they are just waking to the possibility. Some people realize quite early in life that alcohol or drugs are a problem for them and just stop. Others, like me, continue to use, become dependent, and only see the problem when it hits us in the face.

One night I was typing a kind of email to a friend. She was concerned about my drinking, and questioned me about it. I typed the words: "I only drink every night, and only to oblivion." It was one of those "where the hell did that come from" moments. I typed the words without conscious thought, but there they were, out there where I could not ignore them, and the worst part was they were true. In spite of that "revelation," I drank for another six months.

I convinced myself that all the pain I was in and all of my problems were due to my wife, my family, my job, and just about everything in my life, except me. I made plans to escape.

The day after that confrontation with my daughter, I had lunch with my best friend at the Lighthouse Inn in New London, Connecticut. At 2:30 in the afternoon, over my last vodka martini (on the rocks with a twist) I told him that perhaps there was a possibility that maybe I was drinking just a little too much. He told me I should checkout AA because he had heard it was a place I could learn to drink normally. It isn't, of course, but I didn't realize that when I went there for the first time.

A couple of days later, I knew that I was through drinking. It wasn't worth it; I had had enough! I reached the point that professionals call "Crystallization of Discontent," meaning I saw the connection between the booze, the pain, and the problems. For the first time, I realized the downside of drinking far outweighed any benefit I was getting from it.

I did not understand it then, but I had moved from the precontemplative, through the contemplative, and into the action stage in the space of a few days. It took me just 26 years to get there. What I remember about those first few days was a feeling of tremendous relief that perhaps the long nightmare was finally over.

Addiction is a complex issue and we never know what will bring us, or another person, to the point where they question their substance use. For some, prison isn't enough, for others, an off-hand remark from a total stranger might do it. All we can do is have compassion for those who cannot yet see the problem, and not enable them, or interfere with their being able to see it for themselves. That can be very hard to do, especially if it is someone you care about. They will see their situation clearer if we allow them to face the consequences of their actions.

Contemplators – the pros and cons

In all the surveys and studies I referenced in Chapter 2, the number one reason they quit was that they no longer considered the activity "worth it." Using was too much hassle, too much trouble, and was causing them too much discomfort and pain, relative to the benefits they were receiving. As it was their number one reason, it was also their number one motivation for self-change.

There are those with substance dependency problems who move through this stage very rapidly, but many others linger here for years before they decide that the costs of their addictions outweigh any benefits they might be receiving from the drug. To those who have never experienced addiction, the decision to quit seems like it would be an easy one, but to the addict it is not. The drug brings relief, in the short term, for what is for some, unbearable pain. The benefits of not using are more long-term, and that is the problem. The decision involves shifting one's focus from the short-term gratification gained by feeding the habit to the achievement of long-term goals. In other words, the decision necessary to move from stage two to stage three is, in many ways, a decision to grow up.

Preparation

At this stage, you have decided that the benefits of making a change outweigh those of continuing along the same path. Done with the "why," you are now considering the "how." The good news is there are many choices available, and, if you are convinced that you want to change, most of them will work for you. The bad news is that if you are still wrestling with the decision to quit, some of the available choices may do you more harm than good. As I mentioned earlier, these stages are flexible, and people often drift back and forth between them.

During this phase, you will be deciding which of the available methods you will choose to begin the process, but no decision you make here is irrevocable. You can always revisit it depending upon how your chosen method is working out for you. You will base your decision upon a critical, sometimes painful self-evaluation of your degree of dependency, and how you believe you will respond to the different change methods.

Action – getting to work

Congratulations, you have made your decision, not only to make a change but also the method you are going use to do it, and you feel some relief. A weight is off your shoulders, and you feel free to move ahead. Of course, apprehension and a touch of fear are normal at this stage. After all, you have made a decision to leave your "lover," purchased the tickets and are at the airport about to leave!

For some, the last few stages are a complete blur, as they pass from precontemplation to action in a very short time. When I left for work the day I quit, my wife had no inkling that I was going to come home and tell her I was through drinking, but that's what happened.

For most of those who quit on their own, the action stage consisted of a strong resolution to stop using, followed by self-discovery of methods of change that worked for them, including some or all of the following:

- Changes in daily routine

- Engagement in new activities

- Changes in work environment

- Avoidance of situations that created temptation

- A "self-identity" change, that is, saw themselves as a non-user.

- Stopped seeing former "using buddies," and replaced them with non-using new friends

- Terminated unhealthy relationships, even spousal ones when they threatened recovery

- Found and nurtured a new "self-awareness" either through meditation, religious, spiritual, or cognitive means.

- Concentrated upon long-term goals rather than short-term gratification

Most of the recovery programs and self-help groups recommend many of the techniques I just listed, to varying degrees. I suggest you might consider what has worked for those who quit on their own, as they represent the large majority of those who successfully recovered from drug or alcohol dependency. Studies tell us they all used some form or degree of the following:

1. They made a conscious decision that the benefits of not using outweighed the costs (physical, emotional, financial, etc.) of using, thereby gaining the motivation to quit.

2. They had to deal with the urges associated with stopping any drug, the "gotta have its."

3. They had to learn how to get along on a day-to-day basis without resorting to drugs they were using to deal with stress, kill pain, and alter reality, while facing the same problems we all face.

4. They had to learn to balance short and long-term goals, achieve a happy lifestyle, get along with others, in short, learn how to live.

Maintenance – learning to live

After a few months of action in your chosen method, you're starting to feel good about yourself. You're learning to accept yourself unconditionally, and you're practicing long-term goal setting. Your emphasis here is in making the new thought processes you are learning a part of you so that using is not something you can do any longer. You are becoming a different person, and life without your drug of choice is something you cannot only conceive of, but you are actually planning it.

Relapse prevention is a key in this stage. You are building

healthy relationships with others and you are seeking support from an ever-growing circle of friends and acquaintances. You don't want to return to your "old life," and are learning to make the changes within yourself that will make a return at least unlikely, if not impossible. During this stage, most realize that they have not had an urge to use for quite a while. Oh, the thought might pass through their head, but before it becomes an urge it vanishes, sent on its way by a chuckle, or a satisfied smile.

It is not urges that are the biggest danger here, but learning how to deal with the frustrations of life. As we discussed in an earlier chapter, the biophysical part of becoming substance dependent changes your dopamine response, and limbic system, forever. As an ex-addict, you are more susceptible to the stresses of everyday life than are those who were never dependent. We learn to deal with this by changing our thought process, which alters our belief system and keeps our stress level down.

It's not life's "boulders" that drive addicts to relapse; it's the cumulative effect of the "pebbles" we encounter on a daily basis. Each little resentment, each little "she should do this," or "he shouldn't say that," or "this should be this way" is what does us in. "Must," "have to" and "should" beliefs are what we are learning to control at this stage because getting them under control will go a long way towards preventing relapse.

Relapse

Relapse is not a requirement in any recovery program I am aware of. If you have decided that abstinence is your goal, a relapse, or "slip" is not an excuse for an extended period of using. In addition, it is not a reason for you to indulge in self-reproach or guilt. You are learning new skills, a new way of living, and sometimes, in spite of our best efforts, we make mistakes. If properly handled, mistakes are sometimes very valuable learning experiences.

Relapsing when one has been sober for a time is always a choice, always. Most relapses occur in the first five years of recovery, with the vast majority occurring in the first year, principally within the first three months. This is the period when we can stay sober on the strength of the resolution that moved us into the action phase to begin with.

We are beginning to use the tools of the method we have chosen, and are experimenting with a new way of living. While we are learning to accept ourselves as worthwhile human beings, it is very important that we do not let a single setback, or even a series of them, derail us. We consider setbacks as a possibility that could happen as part of the natural change cycle we are going through.

In any case, a slip or relapse is *not* a valid excuse to declare your change attempt a failure and give up. Rather, you might examine the experience with an eye towards what caused it: what the precipitating events were, what were your beliefs about them, and why the beliefs may have been irrational. Sometimes you have to go back and examine your motivation. Perhaps something is still lurking in your mind that sees a long-term advantage to continuing to use. It doesn't matter what your conclusion is, as long as you learn from the experience.

If your chosen method includes a group, either face-to-face or on-line, discuss your slip honestly with others; bring it up yourself, before they ask. Listen; really listen, to the feedback you get. Often others see and recognize things that we do not. We must be open to perceptions that might be hard for us to accept, especially when they contradict things that we "know" to be true about ourselves, or the world around us.

Termination: Moving on

I wish Prochaska and DiClemente had used the word "graduation," but there is a point at which you will become an ex-user and go on with your life. I am aware that 12-step groups contend that you can never stop going to meetings, but available studies do not support that. Three-quarters of recovered substance abusers never went to more than one or two 12-step meetings in their entire lives, and they did just fine.

Most recovered substance abusers worked at a program, either self-directed or with help, for periods ranging from nine to twenty-four months, with the average being about eighteen months. Some people enjoy working with others, and continue doing that with their chosen support groups. They start new meetings; facilitate meetings, etc. just for the satisfaction that working with others brings. A few write books, but most just go on with their lives as productive men and women.

Chapter 5: Tools of Decision

Discovering you might have a problem

I didn't bother to write a chapter for pre-contemplatives because what's the point. Number one, they wouldn't buy the book; and number two, they won't listen to anybody. I know I wouldn't.

Until I woke up the morning after the incident with my daughter, I had no idea I had a problem with alcohol. People told me I did, even people I barely knew. Hell, I even told myself when I wrote a friend that I "only drink every night, and only to oblivion." That's because the only time I didn't feel pain was when I was asleep or passed out. At no time did I ever connect the pain I was in to the alcohol I was drinking—never! Something has driven you to these pages. Could it be the pain of living the way you are? Was it a loved one who delivered an ultimatum? Or are you just sick and tired of being sick and tired? Whatever the reason, you're going to benefit from not only my experience, but also the experience of millions of other people who walked a similar path.

Did I say path? There are as many paths to recovery as there are people who successfully recovered. We each choose a different way, finding the tools and methods that serve our needs the best. I cannot tell you which of the available tools you will find most useful in your own journey—you must discover them for yourself, through trial and error. There are certain tools and methods that seem to work for most, and that's where we will spend the bulk of our time. Even then, a tool that works for one may not work for another.

This chapter is about the "Contemplation" phase of the Stages of Change. The goal is to help you make the decision to change, if you decide that's what is best for you, and suggest things that might help motivate you to continue along the path. Change is not easy, especially when we are considering modifying behaviors we believe are a major part of who we are. If we lack the motivation to change, we do not have much chance of success.

Please do not let the tools in this chapter pin a label on you, or put you in a box. If you should decide, for instance, that you have a drinking problem, it does not mean that you should see yourself as an "alcoholic." Do not allow a single trait, or even a combination of traits to define you in your own mind. The healthy view is to see yourself as a person who has an addictive problem, whether the problem is booze, other drugs, food, sex, or anything else. Do not allow it to define you, for that accomplishes nothing but to give you a built-in reason to fail, a ready-made justification for relapse.

The problem with the term "alcoholic" is not the term itself, the problem is with the "disease model" of alcoholism as promulgated by AA, and the other 12-step groups. AA has coupled the "disease concept" with the principle of "powerlessness" in the mind of the public, and thus created a "disease model" that makes recovery more difficult for most, and increases the incidence of relapse.

As you proceed, watch for attempts by your own mind to put you in a box, and define you according to a subjective set of circumstances.

A risk assessment

How can we tell if we have an addictive problem? The easy answer to that question, and one that has served me well over the years is simply this: is drinking, other drug use, or whatever behavior that brought you to these pages causing a problem in your life? If the answer to that question is yes, than you may have a problem with that substance or behavior.

Let me explain what I mean. Most people, over 85% of the population, can drink when they want to, stop when they want to, and stay away from it when they want to. They don't think about it when they aren't doing it, they don't plan their next binge, they don't take drinking into consideration when they make their plans, and they don't worry about running out. In short, alcohol not only causes no problems in their lives, it is not a concern at all.

There are people who can smoke a cigarette or two a day and even some who can "recreationally" use cocaine, heroin, and other "hard" drugs. The overwhelming majority of us can use prescription drugs as intended, not only narcotics, but other drugs as well. Most people have normal sex lives and eating habits, and they do not gamble away their life savings.

The hardest part of recovery from any addictive behavior can be recognizing it in the first place. We all started out with a particular worldview, in which we saw ourselves as normal, competent people able to make healthy choices and avoid problems. As we slid into addiction, our worldview didn't change with the situation. As our addictive behaviors caused more and more problems, we continued to see this "new normal" as just plain normal. We dealt with any mental discomfort that resulted by ignoring any evidence from the outside world that our behavior was anything but a normal response to circumstances. The people around us created any problems we admitted to having.

You come here hoping to put the question to rest. Do you "have a problem," or don't you? If you've come far enough in the realization process to be honest with yourself, you might find out. I didn't make the following assessments up, by the way; they are both internationally recognized. The first one, known as CAGE-AID, consists of only four yes-or-no questions.

1. Have you ever felt you should Cut down or stop drinking or using drugs?

2. Have people Annoyed you by criticizing you for your drinking or drug use?

3. Have you ever felt bad or Guilty about your drinking or drug use?

4. Have you ever had a drink or used drugs first thing in the morning to steady your nerves or to get rid of a hangover (Eye-opener)?

How did you do? Did you score one yes? Two? The way to score this very accurate test is one "yes" means there is an 80% chance you may be addicted. Two "yes" answers and the odds go up to 89%. Three or more, and it's nearly certain that you have an addictive problem.

This next assessment, called the AUDIT test, is primarily for alcohol addiction, and as that is the most common addiction after nicotine, I included it here. It has ten questions, each scored differently. You can either do this test on a plain piece of paper, or keep a running total of your score in your head as you go through it.

To correctly answer some of these questions you need to

know the definition of a drink. For this test one drink is:

One can of beer (12 oz. or approx. 330 ml of 5% alcohol), or

One glass of wine (5 oz. or approx. 140 ml of 12% alcohol), or

One shot of liquor (1.5 oz. or approx. 40 ml of 40% alcohol).

1. How often do you have a drink containing alcohol?

Never (score 0)

Monthly or less (score 1)

2-4 times a month (score 2)

2-3 times a week (score 3)

4 or more times a week (score 4)

2. How many alcoholic drinks do you have on a typical day when you are drinking?

1 or 2 (0)

3 or 4 (1)

5 or 6 (2)

7-9 (3)

10 or more (4)

3. How often do you have six or more drinks on one occasion?

Never (0)

Less than monthly (1)

Monthly (2)

Weekly (3)

Daily or almost daily (4)

4. How often during the past year did you drink more or for a longer time than you intended?

Never (0)
Less than monthly (1)
Monthly (2)
Weekly (3)
Daily or almost daily (4)

5. How often during the past year have you failed to do what was normally expected of you because of your drinking?
Never (0)
Less than monthly (1)
Monthly (2)
Weekly (3)
Daily or almost daily (4)

6. How often during the past year have you had a drink in the morning to get yourself going after a heavy drinking session?
Never (0)
Less than monthly (1)
Monthly (2)
Weekly (3)
Daily or almost daily (4)

7. How often during the past year have you felt guilty or remorseful after drinking?
Never (0)
Less than monthly (1)
Monthly (2)
Weekly (3)
Daily or almost daily (4)

8. How often during the past year have you been unable

to remember what happened the night before because of your drinking?
Never (0)
Less than monthly (1)
Monthly (2)
Weekly (3)
Daily or almost daily (4)

9. Have you or anyone else been injured as a result of your drinking?
No (0)
Yes, but not in the past year (2)
Yes, during the past year (4)

10. Has a relative, friend, doctor, or health care worker been concerned about your drinking or suggested that you cut down?
No (0)
Yes, but not in the past year (2)
Yes, during the past year (4)

The World Health Organization, an agency of the United Nations, developed this audit and it is in the public domain.

How did you do this time? A score of eight or more indicates that your drinking is potentially hazardous and harmful, with the level of danger rising with the score. A score between 8 and 18 indicates drinking at above healthy levels, and the recommendation is reducing or stopping. A higher score indicates dangerous drinking and possible alcohol dependence; you might consider a significant change.

Again, the object here isn't to put you in a box, the object is to help you with an honest assessment of your addiction problem, or lack of one, if that turned out to be the case.

Determining your values

This simple exercise takes no special training or skills. On a clean sheet of paper, write down the values that are important to you. Don't try to put them in any particular order, just write them down as you think of them. They could be groups of people, like friends and/or family. They could be traits like loyalty, honesty, or professionalism. Whatever they are, they are yours, and there are no right or wrong answers, so write them all down.

When you're done with your list (and it can be as short or comprehensive as you like) make a short list of the five values, from those on your list, that are the most important to you. Again, write them down in no particular order.

Okay, now you should have a list of your top five values on the paper in front of you. Where is your addiction on that list? Notice it is not one of your top five values. Why is it then that you are willing to put your addictive problem in front of all these other values that you say are the most important things on earth to you? Consider the implications of that.

Each time you indulge in your behavior, you put all the things you value at risk. You put your behavior in front of friends, family, job, and all of the other things you hold dear. Why do you do that?

Take that list, your top five, and put it somewhere you will see it all the time. Perhaps on your mirror in the bathroom, maybe on the refrigerator (especially if your problem is an eating disorder), tape it to your PC monitor, keep it in your wallet. The more annoying it is the better.

These are your most important values, and your list will

help in maintaining the motivation for change to keep your highest values in front of you, and in the forefront of your mind, as much as possible. This is most important during the early phases of your recovery efforts.

You might consider revisiting this list on a regular basis. Our values change over time as we grow and mature as people, and a value that made it to your "top five" list six months ago might be number seven now, and something that was not even on the list last year might make it to near the top this year.

As I pointed out in Chapter 3, our minds are plastic, and we become different people over time. Maintaining a "top five values" list is one important way to keep track of these changes, and provide ourselves with a practical method of measuring the progress we're making along the way.

Is using worth it?

We put up with a lot for our addictions, although we seldom realize just how much until we quit. I know that, in my case, I never questioned what my addictions were costing me. Why should I? Things were normal as far as I was concerned, and I would get out of the "situations" I was in just as soon as all of the misconceptions and misunderstandings could be cleared up.

I didn't experience any of the physical or legal problems others did, and I'm not sure it would've made a difference. After all, I would still have quite a few people in my life about whom I could say, "I'll quit if I ever get as bad as _____." No matter how far down the scale we go, there are others worse off, and we're experts at finding them and comparing ourselves to them.

I hope that you've reached the position where you are questioning your using and concerned about the effects, concerned enough to be honest in deciding if using is still worth it to you. After all, you are the only one who can make that decision. Our loved ones can rant and rave, our employers with their pinched faces and thin blue lips can warn us as much as they like, the legal system can threaten us with removal of our license to drive and even our liberty, yet none of that makes any difference until *we* decide that using is not worth it to *us*.

At this point you're probably thinking that you've already made the decision, and that's why you're reading this. However, I suspect you're also feeling just a bit of ambiguity, a little fear and uncertainty, and why shouldn't you? You are considering a major life change, and you don't really know what's ahead. You are looking for a little more certitude, perhaps hard evidence that the course you're considering is indeed the right one for you at this point in your life.

The good news is that I'm about to introduce you to a tool that you're already familiar with, although you may not have seen it presented this way. The bad news is that you must be honest with it, brutally honest. This tool has been around for hundreds if not thousands of years under several different names, but we're going to call it the Cost Benefit Analysis, or CBA.

The CBA is a variation of what you might know as the "Ben Franklin" method of decision making, where old Ben would divide a piece of paper into two columns, and write his reasons for doing something (pros) in one column, and his reasons for not doing something (cons) in the other. Then, with all the reasons for and against in front of him, he would make his decision based upon which side of the paper made the best case.

We use this method, usually without thinking about it, every time we make any decision, from what outfit to wear, what to eat for dinner, or what movie to watch.

We are going to add a level of complexity to the "Franklin" method because we are going to be looking at pros and cons for both using and not using. Yes, there *are* pros for using, just as there are cons for not using. Some of the pros for using are imaginary, as we shall see, but they are real to us just the same. Ignoring them would be the wrong thing to do; it would look as though we were "cooking" the data to make it come out a certain way.

We'll start by taking a sheet of paper, and dividing it in half with a line down the middle. Then we'll divide it in half again, with a horizontal line, so we end up with a big "plus" sign. Above the left quadrant, write "Pros," and above the right quadrant, write, "Cons." In the top half, over to the left side, write "Using," and in the bottom half, write, "Not using." You should end up with something that looks like the worksheet on the next page. You can also find these worksheets on my website, http://powerlessnolonger.com.

Begin filling it in, starting with the pros for using. Sure you have some. You enjoy the buzz; using helps you cope with the world, reduce your anxiety, and it relieves social tension. There are others, but I just wanted to get you started. As you fill out that section, note whether the effect is short or long-term. I will explain why that's important later.

When you're done, move over to the cons of using. Here will be things like hangovers (short-term), legal problems (short and long-term), health problems, etc.. You get the drift. Try to be honest, write down as many as you can, and don't forget to note if they're short or long-term.

COST BENEFIT ANALYSIS

Date: _____

Substance or Activity: _____

<u>Using</u>

<u>Pros</u>   <u>Cons</u>

<u>Not Using</u>

<u>Pros</u>   <u>Cons</u>

Label each item short term or long term

Move to the pros and cons of not using. The pros of not using may be hard, at first, especially if you've not thought much about them. A good place to start might be that many of the pros for not using are the reverse of the cons for using.

Take legal problems, for instance. One of the pros for not using might be that it would be highly unlikely for you to get another DUI if you didn't use anymore, but that's just an example, I'm sure that you can come up with quite a few if you put your mind to it. As before, note if they are short or long-term.

Now, move along to the cons for not using. Yes, there will be a few, and they will mostly be the converse of what you noted under pros for using.

When you're done with this exercise, share it with others. You might even ask for suggestions from those you live with, if they are supportive of this effort. They might suggest things you haven't thought of. You can perform this operation on any addictive behavior or habit you wish. It is a motivational tool, and one that we will return to later, as we progress.

Look at your completed CBA. Note how many of the pros for using are short term, compared with the number of long term cons. Do the same for not using. What do you discover?

I suggest you keep this exercise. Put the paper somewhere safe, so you can pull it out in six months, to see what has changed. When most people examine this exercise after a few months of abstinence, they find that many of the things they listed as pros for using were no longer necessary or important in their lives, and they're usually able to list many more pros for not using then they did before.

Crystallization of Discontent/Desire

The CBA exercise focused upon awareness of the existence of a problem, to introduce a concept called the *crystallization of discontent.* That is what happens when we realize that the negative consequences of continuing a behavior outweigh the positive benefits gained from the behavior. This is a "problem avoidance" approach to motivation, rather than one geared more to the desires of the person considering change. In other words, the CBA focuses upon reasons for running from rather than moving towards.

The second approach, the *crystallization of desire*, is what happens when the person considering change realizes that the positive benefits of changing a behavior outweigh the negatives of continuing the old behavior. In other words, knowing what you want rather than what you don't want.

Both approaches are valid, and both can work, depending upon the person. The important thing is to delineate the reasons why we want to change, and to do it in writing. Once it's "out there," it becomes almost impossible to ignore. For many of us, it's meaningful to do the same for the carrot as we have just done for the stick. The CBA does address some aspects of this approach, but now we are going to focus on what we want.

Take out another piece of paper, and answer the following three questions:

1. What are the changes I want to make?
2. What are the most important reasons I want to make these changes?
3. How do I envision my life in five years?

The first question will be easy for you once you've completed the CBA, but the second question isn't what you might think it is. I'm not looking for answers like "it will keep me out of jail," I'm looking for what staying out of jail will allow you to accomplish. In other words, if you quit drinking, or smoking, for instance, what will you do with all that extra time? What will the differences be in your quality of life? Did you ever consider that?

The last question is the hardest of all, if you do it right. Where do you think you'll be in five years without your addictive behavior? What will you be doing? Where will you be going? What will your daily life be like? Will you go to school, learn a new profession, move to another part of the country or world? Let your mind open up and roam freely through the many possibilities.

I dreamed all the time, when I was drinking, of all the wonderful things I was going to do, but of course I never did any of them—until I quit. Look at your dreams, and realize that you may be on the threshold of realizing them, whatever they may be. I'll guarantee you one thing, based upon many years of observing recovering people: if you do it right, your dreams won't even come close to what you'll achieve.

Motivation – the key to success

This chapter has been about helping you make the decision to change, and suggesting motivational tools to help you get started. Motivation is the single most important ingredient in the behavior modification process. With proper motivation, almost any procedure or method will work, but without it, nothing will. In my own case, for drinking, it was a chain of circumstances over six months culminating in the scene with my daughter in Chapter 1. My motivation for quitting smoking came from two outside influences acting upon me at the same time.

I had a third addictive behavior that I did not identify

until five years ago. I was a long-time day-trader in the stock market, and considered it investing. One night, someone with a self-admitted gambling problem came to my SMART meeting in Wilmington, and I realized that he and I shared many of the same behaviors. I wasn't investing, I was gambling, pure and simple, and for the same reasons he was. We were both adrenalin junkies, and we both used the same irrational justifications. The day after I recognized this in myself, I closed my account. In this instance, it was mere recognition of an addictive problem that provided the motivation to quit.

We never know what it will take for a given person and circumstance, so I've introduced as many different tools as possible, in the hope that one or more of them might hit home. We will see these tools again in the pages ahead, and I encourage you to save the exercises once they are completed. Not only to enhance motivation as we continue, but to mark your progress as you advance along the path because very often our priorities change, and the things we think are important sometimes lose their importance as we grow and mature as individuals.

In the next chapter, you will learn the most effective techniques for changing addictive behaviors, and you will see that many of the top performing modalities involve little other than motivation.

Chapter 6: Preparation

Going about change

After completing the exercises in the last chapter, you're fired-up, ready to go and start changing something, and you're wondering what I'm doing with a chapter called "Preparation." Why do I have to prepare, you might be thinking, why can't I just quit whatever I'm doing and be done with it? Well, of course you can. The first thing anyone has to do to stop addictive behavior is…well…to stop it!

Sounds like a simple statement, but you would be surprised how many people fail to "get it." In my early years in recovery, I'd sit in an AA meeting, and hear people who had obviously been drinking say things like, "Boy, I finally got a bed in a treatment center, I can't wait." As if walking through the magic doorways would solve all their problems.

Another favorite was listening to people at their first AA meeting (or first this time), saying, in effect, "Here I am, let the healing begin," as though there was a 'laying on of hands' ceremony that could zap them sober.

You might laugh, but scenes like that happened on a regular basis. These people could not grasp the simple fact that to stop drinking, they had to…stop drinking. I know I'm belaboring the point, but I'm doing it for a reason. If you do not stop doing whatever brought you to these pages, you will never stop doing it. That's a promise, perhaps the only one in this entire book.

Having said that, let me go a little further, and say that if you don't change your belief system, the chances are that your recovery efforts will not be successful for very long. You don't need any preparation to quit, but you do need a plan as to how you are going to go about modifying your belief system. It will be a lot easier to undertake this planning process if you are not engaged in the behavior that brought you here. Consider that the very best thinking of which you're capable put you where you are today. Things are going so well for you in every aspect of your life that you are considering changing or modifying significant portions of it.

Success in this effort depends upon you and you alone. No one will come riding in to save you from yourself; it is completely up to you. That's the downside. The upside is that it is completely up to you, meaning you have full control of the method you will adapt, and the outcome of your own recovery.

My job is to help you plan your path by first taking a comprehensive look at what works for addiction, according to the latest scientific studies. Then, we will consider the effects your recovery might have upon others, with an emphasis on primary relationships. In the next chapter, we will explore the various recovery groups, comparing their methods with what works. Before moving on, we will create a change plan, detailing where you are, where you would like to go, what your plan is, who can help you, how you can measure your success, and finally, how important it is to you that you achieve it.

Once again, you do not have to wait until your plan is complete. Feel free to stop the behavior now or at least reduce it. This plan will be a lot better if you don't try to do it under the influence, or while you're engaging in the behavior.

What works

There are many studies about what methods and programs work in overcoming addictive behavior. If I were starting from scratch, I would cite hundreds and hundreds of them, weight them, and find a suitable format to present the results so that they made sense to you. I do not have to—someone already did.

Psychologists at the University of New Mexico, led by Dr. William Miller, tabulated every controlled study of alcoholism treatment they could find. They weighted each study based upon the quality of its research methodology, to arrive at a comprehensive list, which they first published in book form in 1995 and have continually updated. They call the book *Handbook of Alcoholism Treatment Approaches: Effective Alternatives.*

Notice that these studies addressed addiction to alcohol, not any other drugs. However, we are modifying addictive behaviors here, and they are virtually identical across the entire range of habits and substances.

In Miller's list, three of the top ten are drugs themselves. They are Acamprosate, which reduces urges and cravings, Naltrexone, which blocks the euphoric effects of alcohol and certain narcotics, and Antabuse, which produces nausea if alcohol is consumed. Acamprosate is still under study for use in the United States, while Naltrexone and Antabuse have been available for a while. If you are under a doctor's care, or involved in a program that uses one of these drugs, follow whatever guidelines you've been given.

Exclusive of the three drugs mentioned above, the top ten modalities are: [43]

- Brief interventions
- Motivational enhancement
- Community reinforcement (CRA)
- Self-change manual (Bibliotherapy)
- Behavioral self-control training
- Behavior contracting
- Social skills training
- Marital therapy-behavioral
- Case management
- Cognitive therapy

Let us look at these one at a time:

1. **Brief Intervention** — A discussion with a trusted medical person, usually a family doctor or other professional. One of our problems as addicts is that we are seldom honest with medical people when discussing our usage patterns. When we are, it's often an indication that we are ready, or almost ready, to make a change. I quit smoking this way because of a brief discussion with my cardiologist.

2. **Motivational Enhancement** — Also known as Motivational Interviewing, this program consists of a thorough assessment of drug use, risk factors, family history, drug related problems, level of dependence, and motivation. The key in this approach is that it helps you see the good and bad things about your drug use, to help you resolve any lingering ambivalence about changing your behavior.

3.   **Community Reinforcement Approach (CRA)** — CRA is a treatment approach that works by eliminating positive reinforcement for using and enhancing positive reinforcement for sobriety. It integrates several treatment components, including building motivation to quit, analyzing using patterns, increasing positive reinforcement, teaching new coping skills, and involving significant others in the recovery process. It shares many components with the motivational enhancement programs.

4.   **Self-Change Manuals (Bibliotherapy)** — *Powerless No Longer* falls into this category. A significant number of addicts recover because of what they learn from these manuals. Some of them concentrate on moderation rather than abstinence, and many more address various phases of the 12-step approach.

5.   **Behavioral Self-Control Training** — A behavioral program that's based upon the "learning model" of addiction, that I presented in Chapter 3 rather than the "disease model." It is used by those who wish to abstain or those whose goal is moderation. It consists of cognitive behavioral techniques that can be either self-taught, or used in conjunction with other programs or formal therapy.

6.   **Behavior Contracting** — Usually used by therapists, it involves the addict making one or more written contracts concerning their behavior and their goals. The contract spells out the

expectations and the commitments of the addict, the therapist, and in some cases the family of the addict. It is primarily a positive reinforcement tool.

7. **Social Skills Training** — Programs which use a cognitive-behavioral approach to change the behavior patterns of addicts, especially in the area of getting along with the rest of the world. Kind of a Kindergarten for recovering addicts.

8. **Behavioral Marital Therapy** — Geared to married couples, this method, used by therapists, involves a contract not to use, and a series of behavioral assignments. It assumes that intimate partners can reward abstinence, and that reducing relationship tension reduces the risk of relapse.

9. **Case Management** — Not really a therapy, case management is a set of interventions aiming to facilitate the treatment outcome. Some of the functions are providing individualized support, helping the addict solve problems, helping with employment issues, etc.. In short, making sure there is a support system around recovery.

10. **Cognitive Therapy** — This is a large, catchall category that includes Cognitive Behavioral Therapy, Rational Emotive Behavioral Therapy, and several others. Many of the programs and methodologies above use cognitive therapies as part of their procedures, but this category looks at cognitive therapy alone, and not in conjunction with other methodologies.

In Chapter 1, I listed four factors that were common in

most successful recoveries. They were motivation, dealing with urges, problem solving, and balancing short and long-term goals. Table 1 below lists the "top ten" recovery modalities, and which of the four points they address.

As you can see, seven of the modalities deal with motivation, five with urges, eight with problem-solving, and three give some insight into balancing short and long-term goals. Only one of the treatment modalities addresses all four of the factors, but that does not mean that every self-help book on the market is that comprehensive. Some are narrow in focus, while others, such as this one, offer a broad range of suggestions.

Treatment Modality	1	2	3	4
Brief intervention	X			
Motivational enhancement	X			
CRA	X	X	X	
Manual	X	X	X	X
Behavioral self-control		X	X	X
Behavior contracting	X		X	
Social skills			X	X
Marital therapy – behavioral	X	X	X	
Case management	X		X	
Cognitive therapy		X	X	

Table 1

So where are we? The data tell us that to have the best chance of success, any recovery program should include the modalities and methods indicated above, but how can we determine what would work best for ourselves? For some of us the choices can seem overwhelming, and we might wonder if there is a guide or road map we could use to make them clearer.

Fortunately, there is, and I introduced it in the last chapter. The Stages of Change can serve as our GPS as we navigate through the labyrinth of available recovery choices. There are tools suggested by the various stages, and the tools are independent of the recovery modalities.

In the first chapter, I promised to disclose what methods actually work for people who have problems with addictive behavior. Well, here they are, and the rest of the book is about putting these methodologies to work on your problem, whatever it might be.

Considering effects upon others

We do nothing in a vacuum. We all have spouses, significant others, parents, relatives, or co-workers who are affected by our behaviors. The vast majority of the people in our lives will be supportive of our efforts to change, but that is not always the case. If we have tried to change in the past, and the effort became another in a long line of learning experiences, they have heard it all before, and might just respond with "There he/she goes again."

Some of us have spouses or significant others who were "drinking buddies," and we cannot expect them to join the cause, particularly if the relationship has been a long-term one. We have to remember that any change is scary, not just to us, but sometimes to those around us as well.

If we are successful in our change process, we are going to become different people. It is inevitable. Our values, priorities, habits, and our behaviors will change. Some of those closest to us may feel threatened by these changes, especially if our new habits and outlook preclude activities that we used to share. If we are trying to quit drinking, for instance, and our habit was to go out for an evening of revelry with our spouse every now and then, that might not happen any longer. If we used to meet our friends after work on Friday night for a "few pops," that might not be advisable any more.

Nothing I can think of is more boring than hanging around with people who are drinking if you happen to be sober. You can only listen for so long to the same old stories, told in the same old ways, and the same old dreams presented in the same old manner. You will wonder how you ever did this for so long.

The most serious situation, and the one that can be hardest to resolve, is the case of two people living together who both use, and one of them quits. These relationships often have serious flaws, but sometimes hang together as long as the status quo is preserved. One partner deciding they have "had enough" is sometimes enough for the other to become aware of their own problem, but sometimes not. If not, and one partner follows through with their recovery plan, this could put a serious strain on an already tense relationship.

If you are in that situation, try to be somewhat sympathetic to the position in which you've placed your spouse or significant other. From their point of view things were far from perfect, but at least you shared certain areas of your lives together, even if it was only while you were both using. You went to parties with friends who used, and chances are you long ago filtered your friends into two classes—those who drank (or used) and those who didn't. Your vacations revolved around drinking or using. In short, your lives together were just as centered on substances or behaviors as an individual addict's life—you just did it together, or at least in relative proximity.

Now, because of a decision *you* have made, their lives are turned totally upside down. They have lost their drinking buddy, their excuse to use, and perhaps their best method of controlling you. They cannot help but resent the person who is shining the "holier than thou" spotlight upon them, whether you are or not. In fact, the decision you have made, as far as they're concerned, is all about them, not you. You are not doing this *for* yourself, you are doing it *to* them!

I cannot stress that enough because it's important for you to realize where their attitudes are coming from. It will seem to you that they are being unreasonable and irrational. Perhaps they are, but not to themselves; that's the tragedy of it. If they continue using, they may start doing it in secret, instead of in the open. If you go out to meetings in the evening, they may resent it, along with the new friends you're making. Depending upon the severity of their own problem, they may even try to sabotage your efforts in various ways.

You are very vulnerable in early recovery, for many reasons. Trying to learn new habits and attitudes is not an easy task in the best of times. It is even more difficult when you may be feeling guilty for your part in the earlier problems in the relationship. What you have to remember is that you are not responsible for the feelings or actions of your significant other if they make things difficult for you at this time. They will not stop using if you are a better wife or husband. They will not stop using if you are a better provider. They will not stop using if you forgo your recovery efforts and slip back into your old life together. In short, their using has nothing to do with you, and everything to do with them.

This is a grim picture, and not all recoveries involve situations like this. The ones that do, however, are very difficult indeed for the recovering person. There is no fixed rule as to how these things play out. Some relationships break up when one partner quits, others stay together. One thing is certain: studies prove that many more recoveries are successful when the primary relationship is supportive than when it is not. You have to make your own decision about your own situation, keeping in mind that this is your life and your future.

So, how can you head off problems in this area before they get started? One way is to sit down with everyone involved and frankly discuss your reasons for taking the step you are taking. In the case of a using partner, explain that this decision has little to do with them; it is not because of them, or anything they have or haven't done. It is about *your* health, *your* quality of life, and *your* future. If handled calmly and rationally, there is a good chance they might see their own situation. If you have completed it already, share your CBA with them, emphasizing the pros and cons that relate most strongly to your primary relationships.

Do not allow anyone to draw you into a debate about your addiction. It is easy at this early stage to be swayed by a "but you're not really *that* bad" conversation. A great example of that was my own mother, who loved me dearly and only wanted the best for me. I started drinking in the navy, when I was eighteen. For the next twenty-six years, I saw my mother mostly at family gatherings, holidays, and other special occasions. I never felt comfortable at such occasions without having a couple of drinks, so when I told my mother that I was quitting drinking, she asked me why. From her point of view there was no need, and she told me so. I finally convinced her that from the time I joined the Navy until I quit, she never saw me sober.

Even well-meaning friends and relatives can try to convince us we are not addicts—and this is especially true if they often drank with us. If we pronounce ourselves addicts, they might have to look at themselves, and as you know, that is a very hard thing to do.

Chapter 7: Support Groups

Overview of 12-step

Do you consider yourself a "spiritual" person? If you're not sure what that means, according to the *New Oxford American Dictionary*, it's: "*of, relating to, or affecting the human spirit or soul as opposed to material or physical things; as in: the spiritual values of life.*" For the recovery methods explained in this book, it doesn't matter if you are or not. It *does* matter, if you consider 12-step as one of your recovery choices. It matters because the 12-step programs consider themselves spiritual in nature, and they insist that no recovery is possible without, in the words of co-founder Bill Wilson, "*...getting the spiritual angle...*"

In the interests of full disclosure, it was into an AA meeting that I stumbled in 1990. At the time, there were no other choices. AA was where you went if you had a problem with alcohol. If you had the insurance to cover a period of professional treatment (usually 28 days), what you received there was a 24/7 dose of the same principles. I did none of the things "suggested," but I stayed sober anyway.

I am not going to go into detail on the program or history of AA, for that information is available from many other sources, including AA itself. I will mention a few things because they bear upon the ideas in this book. I will not differentiate between AA and the other 12-step organizations because, even though they are separate, they follow the same steps and adhere to the same principles.

AA was founded in the mid-1930s, by two individuals

with pronounced drinking problems. They started the fellowship in Akron, Ohio as a spin-off of a fundamentalist Christian religious cult known as the Oxford Group. The Oxford Group had some "steps to salvation," based upon the Christian model of original sin and redemption. For instance, the first step of the Oxford Group was, "I am powerless over sin, I am defeated by it." [44]

When Bill Wilson, one of the co-founders of AA wrote *Alcoholics Anonymous* (referred to as the "Big Book") in 1939, he changed the first step to read, *"We admitted we were powerless over alcohol—that our lives had become unmanageable."* The next two steps continued with the redemption model, "coming to believe" that only a "power greater than ourselves could restore us to sanity," and making a decision to "turn our will and our lives over to the care of God *as we understood Him."*

The next six steps follow the religious model, calling for confession of our "sins," asking God to remove our "character defects," and the making of amends to those we had "harmed" while we were using. step 10 is the heart of the program, although most AAs have no idea what it means, and the last two steps call for growing closer to the God of our understanding, and "carrying the message" to other suffering alcoholics. The last is always a good idea, regardless of the program or method you happen to choose.

Is AA a religion? In the legal sense, every Federal court that has looked at the issue has said it is, from the standpoint of sentencing people to attend AA meetings. The courts have ruled that such sentencing violates the separation of church and state called for in the First Amendment. Many of you reading this have attended meetings, what do you think?

It doesn't matter if it's a religion; all that matters is whether it works or not. From an evidentiary standpoint, AA clearly does not work for most people. Yes, I realize that everyone knows "someone" who has been helped by AA, or one of the other 12-step programs, but what does that really mean? According to the first survey of AA efficacy, done by AA itself in 1988-89, the percentage of people who enter AA and are still there, and still sober after one year is 5%. This number has not varied much over the years, no matter who does the measuring or how they do it. [45]

Thousands of people walk through the doors of AA each year, and many of them recover from their addictive problem. The studies presented earlier in this book show that 75% of them would have recovered anyway, so AA's 5% efficacy rate is what you would expect from natural recovery alone. I am a perfect example of that. I started in AA, but I did none of the things it suggested, and I left after a few years. Was AA the instrument of my recovery?

There is considerable evidence that AA is actually harmful to many people, insisting, as it does, that addicts are powerless over their addictions. If one fails to stay sober in AA and believes they are powerless, where do they turn next? If they cannot form a relationship with this "God as we understand him," what chance do they have of ever recovering? *That* is my problem with AA and the disease model of alcoholism.

In his book, *7 Tools to Beat Addiction,* noted addiction researcher, Dr. Stanton Peele points out in Chapter 1:

> *"Psychologist William Miller and his colleagues at the University of New Mexico conducted an important study in which they tracked subjects who reported for outpatient*

treatment for an alcohol problem. The investigators' purpose was to forecast which subjects were more likely to relapse following treatment. They found two primary factors predicted relapse—'lack of coping skills and belief in the disease model of alcoholism.'

"Think of it—treatment in the United States is geared primarily toward teaching people to believe something that makes it more likely that they will relapse! Instead, psychological theory and research indicate that it is more empowering and successful for you to believe in—and to value—your own strength. In this view, the critical element in cure is to develop your sense of self-efficacy. Yet if you express this view, or that you are uncomfortable with the value of powerlessness taught in the twelve-step approach, you will be told that you are in denial and that you cannot succeed at quitting addiction." [46]

There is no clinical evidence that there is any need for spirituality in recovery, although there is evidence that a spiritual approach can be of help to some people. Whether or not you include spirituality in your program is up to you.

AA is a rigid program, in spite of one of their favorite mottos: "take what you need and leave the rest." Most AA members tend to be suspicious of the commitment of those who disregard parts of the program. If you resist being labeled "alcoholic," for instance, you will be accused of being "in denial" of your true condition. If you don't stumble in with a belief in a "power greater than yourself," you will be admonished to "fake it until you make it," meaning you should go through the motions, pretending belief in a higher power, until you magically acquire it.

In spite of placing so low on the "what works" list, (AA

is number 38) and evidence that only 5% of those who try it are successful, there is no doubt that AA and other 12-step groups have been the primary means of recovery for millions of people. This seems, on the surface at least, to be a contradiction. How can a program that has remained unchanged for over seventy years, in spite of all we've learned about addiction, retain such a loyal following, even inside the recovery industry? The answer lies in the huge investment in training within the recovery industry as it exists today. When there's a paradigm shift in any field of knowledge, it takes time for the new ideas to gain traction.

Most of what we know about addiction we've learned in the past 40 years, and much of that since the invention of the fMRI. The first edition of *Alcoholics Anonymous* came out in 1939. In spite of all we now know about addiction, AA has not changed a single word in the first 164 pages of the book, the part that contains the program, in any of the editions published since.

Estimations are that there is at least a 15-year lag between what the research community knows to be true about addiction and how the treatment industry actually treats. Think of an industry with thousands of treatment facilitators, most trained only in the twelve-step method. It takes time, and a tremendous amount of energy, to turn that around.

There is resistance within the industry to the teaching of cognitive techniques, but only part of this is due to forces within the treatment infrastructure. A good deal of the resistance is due to the undeniable public acceptance of 12-step, and that is even harder to overcome.

I have been trying to give you a flavor of the 12-step approach so you can make a determination of whether or not it would work for you. What I have not done thus far is mention some of the positive things about these programs. After all, they've been around for many years, and millions have recovered in their rooms.

When I think about 12-step, the first thing that comes to mind is the fellowship. When I walked through the doors in 1990, I felt safe, as though nothing could harm me as long as I remained within the room. I also sensed a kinship with the people there. I believed that they had been where I was, and if this marvelous thing had worked for them, it could work for me as well. That worked, as long as I was in the room, or somewhere else (like a coffee shop or restaurant) surrounded by 12-step people.

The sensation I'm talking about is that of being "in the center of the herd." It's due primarily to a chemical called serotonin, a neurotransmitter released in the brain when anxiety over a perceived threat is relieved. Admittedly, that is an oversimplification, but it's accurate for this purpose. The neurotransmitter dopamine, released as a response to stress, causes the feeling of anxiety.

We live our daily lives in the real world, with all the challenges and frustrations that everyone faces. These raise our anxiety levels and trigger impulses to engage in our addictive behaviors. When one recognizes the onset of increased anxiety levels that could trigger using, 12-step programs teach that the addict should pray, call another addict, or if possible, get to a meeting.

Any one of the three could lower the addict's anxiety level enough to lessen the threat of using. What happens in the brain is a lowering of the dopamine levels, along with a rise in the levels of serotonin. This of course assumes that the addict is in a position where he can do one of these things, and that the necessary resources are available.

Working the program possibly lowers the frequency of emotional upsets, but it does little to help the addict deal with the normal day-to-day stresses that cause relapse.

I mentioned earlier that step 10 is the heart of the program, although most 12-steppers miss it completely. In Chapter 5 of *Alcoholics Anonymous*, it reads as follows. "*Continued to take personal inventory and when we were wrong promptly admitted it.*" [47] If you ask 12-steppers what that means, most will say it means you take a personal inventory each night upon retiring, and take appropriate action the next day. That is not correct, according to the actual explanation of the step in the next chapter of *Alcoholics Anonymous*. Chapter 6, page 84, admonishes the alcoholic to:

> "*Continue to take personal inventory and continue to set right any new mistakes **as we go along**. ...Continue to watch for selfishness, dishonesty, resentment, and fear. When these crop up, we ask God **at once** to remove them. We discuss them with someone **immediately** and make amends **quickly** if we have harmed anyone.*" [48] [Emphasis mine]

According to the AA-conference-approved "Joe and Charlie" tapes, interpretations of the 12 steps by a couple of "old-timers," step ten means to do steps four, five, six, seven, eight, and nine *in real time*, as we go through our day. [49] In other words, the step is telling us to be present to our lives, and in the moment, observing our own thoughts and behaviors. If we do this, we will eventually begin to recognize those that are irrational, even without a systematic program like the one I advance in this book.

If one were to throw out the entire rest of the 12-step program, and just concentrate on step 10, it would be a more effective program, in my opinion. It would be more effective because it would reflect what we know actually works against addictive behavior.

Twelve-step lore is rich in stories of individuals with long-term abstinence who stop going to meetings and "practicing the program" for short periods of time and relapse, finding themselves in far worse shape than they ever were before. Such instances are evidence that if one simply goes to meetings for years, relies upon the "serotonin fix," and fails to change their attitudes and beliefs, they might achieve long-term sobriety, but in reality they have but a single year of growth repeated many times.

Many others, perhaps the overwhelming majority, stay with 12-step for a few months or years, cease going to meetings or doing any of the other "suggested" things, and go on with their lives in a perfectly normal manner. How does 12-step account for this majority who leave and go on with their lives? Inside the rooms, they say that such people are "in denial," and experiencing miserable lives as "dry drunks." What could be more ridiculous?

Compare this to the cognitive approach this book suggests. If you accept that engaging in your addictive behavior is a choice that you have ultimate control over, you are then responsible for taking the measures necessary to control your own anxiety levels, without invoking the aid of a power greater than yourself, or even another human being. In the terms of an overused cliché, the cognitive approach doesn't give you a fish, feeding you for a day; it teaches you how to fish so you can feed yourself for the rest of your life.

Twelve-step meetings come in many different formats, and the formats vary from area to area, so it's difficult to give a good picture of what constitutes a typical meeting. The "classic" format, the format you see on TV and in the movies, is the speaker meeting. At this meeting, one or more speakers tell their stories, beginning with their early years, and on through their using history. If they have any recovery time, they finish with that. Speakers generally follow the format "what it was like, what happened, and what it's like now." The object is to create a feeling of identification in the newcomer, and remind the speaker of what it used to be like in his or her own life when they were using.

The discussion meeting is another popular format. The leader picks the topic, and anyone who wishes may comment, in serial fashion, with no crosstalk allowed. There are step discussion meetings, tradition meetings that address the traditions of the fellowship, Big Book meetings where *Alcoholics Anonymous* is discussed chapter by chapter, and beginner meetings for newcomers.

Meetings may be "open," allowing non-addicts to attend, or "closed," which are limited to addicts only. There are men's meetings; woman's meetings; and a whole shopping list of other "specialty" meetings for sub-groups of addicts. There are even several atheist and agnostic meetings, although the AA central office is doing what they can to discourage them.

Regardless of the format, most meetings start with those present joining in the "Serenity Prayer," (God, grant me the serenity…). Next, in most meetings, is a reading of "How it Works" from Chapter 5 of *Alcoholics Anonymous,* followed by readings from other 12-step literature, depending upon what the group has decided. Meetings end with everyone present joining hands, and reciting the Christian Lord's Prayer.

None of the approaches in this book are mutually exclusive, and there are as many routes to recovery as recovered people. Very often I suggest to those new in recovery that they could benefit by taking advantage of the fellowship available as part of 12-step meetings.

SMART Recovery®

SMART is an acronym standing for: **S**elf **M**anagement **A**nd **R**ecovery **T**raining; it doesn't mean to say that its acolytes are any "smarter" than other recovering people are. I am presently a SMART meeting facilitator. In 2012, I started a meeting here in the little Mexican village where I live. A therapist who believed there was a need for a secular recovery meeting encouraged me to start it.

This isn't the first meeting I've been involved with, as I helped start a meeting in Wilmington, North Carolina, a few years ago with Mike Werner, one of the founders of SMART.

I want to make it clear, once again, that I do not speak for SMART Recovery®. The opinions expressed in this book are mine and mine alone, and do not necessarily reflect those of SMART or any other recovery organization.

In earlier chapters, I listed the four components of a successful recovery. Once again, they are:

1. Enhancing and maintaining motivation

2. Coping with urges

3. Managing thoughts, feelings, and behaviors (problem solving)

4. Achieving a balance between short and long-term gratification

Those four components are the four points of SMART, an evidence-based program that evolves as scientific knowledge evolves. SMART is a self-empowering program, believing that using is a choice that the addicts ultimately have the power within themselves to control. SMART has a web site (http://smartrecovery.org) and a network of face-to-face meetings all over the world.

SMART offers a complete kit of evidence-based tools. I am not going to go deeply into the program itself here, as many of the tools SMART uses are covered in detail elsewhere in this book. All SMART meetings follow the same basic agenda. There are minor differences between meetings, depending on the presence of newcomers to the program and regional differences.

1. Welcome and opening statement, usually read by the facilitator.

2. Check-in, a personal update, how have the members been since the last meeting. The facilitator goes around the room, and each person briefly covers their successes and/or challenges in the last week.

3. Agenda setting: the facilitator, with the aid of the group, sets the agenda for the rest of the meeting based upon what comes up at the check-in.

4. Working time: coping with activating events, focusing upon the four-point program.

5. Donations: pass-the-hat time.

6.   Check out: meeting review and plans for the week.

The time spent on each of these depends upon the length of the meeting, which is usually 90 minutes. The on-line meetings held on the website follow the same format, although again there may be slight differences depending upon the individual style of the facilitator.

SMART meetings are not as ubiquitous as AA meetings, although the program is experiencing rapid growth. There are meetings in or near most major cities in the United States, as well as many meetings throughout the world. Of course, there are always the on-line meetings available on the SMART web site.

In the *What works* section of Chapter 6, I listed the ten modalities that studies say are most effective against addictive behavior. With a few additions, the appropriate components from this list comprise the SMART program. These components by themselves have a great deal of evidentiary support, but until recently, no one had ever done a scientific study of the SMART program itself.

On June 12, 2013, just days before the publication of this book, the National Institute on Alcohol Abuse and Alcoholism (NIAA) released the results of a randomized clinical study on the effectiveness of SMART Recovery® and an interactive application on the SMART web site called "Overcoming Addictions." The application, which is based on the program, will be available on www.smartrecovery.org beginning in September 2013.

The results of the study, which lasted three months, showed that the 189 participants increased their percentage of days abstinent by as much as 72%, and significantly reduced their alcohol and drug-related consequences. [50] There will be a six-month follow-up, and I will post it on www.powerlessnolonger.com as soon as it is available.

Other support groups

Professionals experienced in the field of recovery from drugs and alcohol practice many of the "top ten" methods from Chapter 6. There is nothing wrong with consulting a professional if you wish to, or if a trusted medical adviser has suggested that you do so. This is not a contest to see who can recover with the least help; this is the rest of your life, and you should be willing to do whatever it takes.

In my own case, I saw a therapist for a time when I first quit drinking, and the experience was very helpful to me. I drew bits and pieces from AA, Zen Buddhism, a couple of self-help books, and finally SMART Recovery®. I cannot credit any one of them, as each played a role. Some of us have problems other than the addictive substance or behavior we engage in, and professionals can be useful to help us work through these problems and sort things out. Sometimes quitting, in and of itself, relieves these problems, but unfortunately sometimes they become worse without the drugs we were using to self-medicate.

I would be the last person to tell you "you need this," or "you don't need that." *Powerless No Longer* is about informing you and giving you choices, not trying to shove any particular method down your throat. Don't let anyone else do that either. Empowerment is informing yourself and making your own choices. What worked for your uncle Al or myself might not work for you.

Many studies in Chapter 2 identified "problem drinkers" who met DSM criteria at one point, and were able to moderate their drinking to the point where they no longer met the criteria, and drinking was no longer causing problems in their lives. Typically, these drinkers were early in the cycle, and had not progressed to the point of alcohol dependence. I am sure that moderation would not work for me, based upon the level of dependence I reached before I stopped, but that does not mean it wouldn't work for you.

There is a formal program, Moderation Management (MM), which addresses this group of problem drinkers. They only address alcohol, not any other drug or addictive behavior. MM holds that alcoholism is not a disease addicts are powerless over, and that cognitive methods can be helpful to drinkers in moderating their behavior. Their program, explained on their web site, begins with 30 days of abstinence, followed by a weekly quota of 14 "standard" drinks a week, with no more than 4 drinks on any particular day. Those limits are for men; women's limits are slightly less. They define their prospective membership of "non-dependent problem drinkers" as anyone who demonstrates the ability to complete the 30 days of abstinence and hold to the guidelines on quantity and frequency.

By mentioning MM, I'm not advocating moderation; that's something that you can decide for yourself—after the 30 days of abstinence the program specifies. So much depends upon your own situation, and the severity of your addiction, that no outside observer could really make that determination. If your problem is alcohol, and if your addiction is not too severe, as measured by the criteria in the *Risk Assessment* section of Chapter 5, you might want to give it a shot. I think you might find, however, that moderation is a lot harder to maintain than abstinence.

Another secular self-help organization is Secular Organizations for Sobriety (SOS), also known as Save Our Selves. This primarily Humanist organization began in 1985, and serves those who are uncomfortable with the religiosity of 12-step organizations. SOS believes in empowering the individual to overcome addiction, rather than relying upon any outside source. There are not as many meetings available as some of the other groups, but they are worth a look if you are considering quitting on your own.

There are other organizations and formal programs that follow the cognitive path to recovery. I have listed as many as I can in the *Resources* section of the appendix, and on the web site for this book.

In recovery, a good plan today is better than a perfect plan tomorrow. Do not let planning keep you from doing the most important thing: stopping the addictive behavior as soon as you can. Regardless of the method you choose your initial goal will be abstinence, and you can begin now. Many of us start with one method or program and move on to others that better fit our needs.

I said earlier, and it bears repeating here: if a person is motivated almost anything will work, but in the absence of motivation, nothing will. That's what makes it easy for us. With good motivation, it almost doesn't matter what we do in the beginning. It is only important that we get off our sinking ship and into a lifeboat as soon as we can; which lifeboat we choose doesn't matter.

As a SMART facilitator, I do not discourage newcomers from attending 12-step meetings, especially if they find comfort in the fellowship. Over the years, I learned that most people find their own way, taking bits and pieces from various programs. I tried to give an accurate picture of some recovery groups in this chapter, but you won't really understand what they are like unless you experience them for yourself. Try not to be guilty of contempt prior to investigation.

I stumbled into AA in 1990 because that's what you did then if you thought you had a drinking problem. At the time there were no secular alternatives, at least that I knew of, and there was no internet. Things are different today, and you have access to all of the recovery programs on the planet.

Investigate all you like, but remember that the important thing is to get off that ship. Don't let anything interfere with that. If you want to stop using, you have to…stop!

Chapter 8: Reprogramming Beliefs

Changing your belief system

In an earlier chapter, we discovered how we learn, retain information, and form habits both good and bad. We learned that the brain forms neural networks based upon our experiences, and that these produce thoughts, beliefs, and actions, both healthy and unhealthy.

Long and frequent usage deeply imbeds our habits and beliefs, and it sometimes seems as though we are powerless to change them. When we combine an intrinsically addictive substance with an unhealthy belief system, the consequences seem impossible to overcome. People just like us do exactly that, however, as we learned in Chapter 2. Perhaps they used the tool I'm about to discuss, but most, like myself, weren't even aware it existed.

We are going to be using this tool throughout the rest of the book, so it makes sense to introduce the main points all in one place. You can refer back to it, if necessary, as you move along. It sounds complicated at first, but once you get the hang of it, it's very simple.

Rational Emotive Behavior Therapy (REBT) is a system of therapy, and a school of thought, established by Dr. Albert Ellis in the mid 1950s. REBT was the first of the cognitive behavioral therapies, and it lends itself well to both professional use and self-help. The basic premise of REBT is that it is how we choose to interpret events, rather than the events themselves, that upsets us. If we're watching a football game and a team scores a touchdown, that's an event. How we interpret the event depends upon which team we happen to be rooting for.

This is not a new philosophy. The "Stoic" school in ancient Greece first expressed these ideas, most notably Epictetus, who wrote in the first century CE, "Men are disturbed not by things, but by the views which they take of them." In other words, it is not the events of daily life that upset us, but our perceptions and interpretations, which form our beliefs about reality.

Most of us want to be happy, not miserable, anxious, or depressed. We want to get along with others, be well-informed, well-educated, have a good job that stimulates us and we want to enjoy our leisure time. Unfortunately, things do not always work out the way we plan them. Sometimes events we have little or no control over keep us from achieving our goals.

Albert Ellis and REBT advance the theory that our beliefs determine our reaction to having our goals blocked. Dr. Ellis developed an *ABC* format to illustrate the process of changing our belief system. The premise of this book is that we can overcome our addictive behaviors by reprogramming our responses to events either inside or outside of ourselves, and here is the way we do this:

A. The Activating event. It can be an actual event, or it can be a thought or idea

B. Your Belief about the activating event—your perception, or belief about the *A*

C. The Consequences of your belief—an emotional or behavioral reaction

An example might be:

A. Your employer calls you into her office and criticizes you for messing up an assignment.

B. You believe you are a failure who will never be able to do your job, and/or will soon be fired, and to lose your job would be unbearable.

C. You are depressed, sorry for yourself, and extremely anxious. When you leave work, you stop at the bar on the way home....

In the REBT model, it is not the *A* that causes the *C,* it is the *B,* or our belief about the *A.* In the example above, it's not the reprimand that caused you to feel depressed, it was your belief that falling short of your employer's expectations on this particular assignment meant you were a failure, would probably soon be fired, and to be fired would be unbearable.

Looking at this example rationally, we can see that not doing well on a single assignment does not make you, or anyone else, a failure. You are not a failure, and using this language to describe yourself is not helpful. Of course you can learn to do your job, and use of the word "never" is irrational. You have no evidence you are going to be fired over this incident, and even if you were, people are fired all the time. The experience, although not pleasant, is bearable. You can see in this example that the beliefs were unhealthy, irrational, and led directly to the consequences.

We express ourselves differently, but the beliefs that upset us are all variations of three common irrational beliefs. Each of these three beliefs contains a demand about ourselves, other people, or the world at large. Collectively, they are known in REBT as *The Three Basic Musts.*

1. I **must** do well and win the approval of others for my performances or else I am no good.

2. Other people **must** treat me considerately, fairly and kindly, and in exactly the way I wish to be treated. If they don't, they are no good and deserve to be condemned and punished.

3. I **must** get what I want, when I want it; and I must not get what I don't want. It's terrible if I don't get what I want, and I can't stand it.

Number one above often leads to anxiety, depression, shame, and guilt. Number two often leads to rage and acts of violence. The third can lead to self-pity and procrastination. The demanding nature of these irrational beliefs causes emotional upset. Less demanding, more flexible beliefs lead to healthy emotions and helpful behaviors.

The goal of REBT is to help you change your irrational beliefs, such as those in the example above, to rational beliefs. We call the process we use to do this *Disputing*, and it becomes the *D* in the REBT *ABC* model. We have learned our current belief system and the behaviors that follow. Disputing the beliefs is the best method to learn new behaviors. If we do nothing about the beliefs and work only on the behaviors, relying upon will power alone, we will increase our risk of relapse.

Disputing beliefs is a two-part process. First, we question the belief to determine if it's rational; and second, we replace the irrational belief with a rational one. The following three questions we can use to test our beliefs are an adaptation of Dr. Maxie C. Maultsby's *Five Criteria for Rational Thinking*.

1. <u>**Is my belief based upon fact?**</u> If we had a camera

recording the scene, would the camera show the scene the same way my thoughts reflect it, or would the image be different? A camera can only record whatever is in front of it, neither adding to nor detracting from the scene. The human brain, on the other hand, does not have that limitation. We can add to, subtract from, or otherwise distort the image, based upon what we already think or believe about what we're seeing. It's important to look at the situation as though we were a camera recording it, perceiving only what's actually happening.

2. **Does my belief help me achieve my short and long-term goals?** Any thought that does not help you achieve your goals, or is contrary to them, would not pass this test. Beliefs such as *"I'll just have one drink,"* when you have plenty of evidence that this is impossible, and your goal is abstinence, would fail this test (and the first test as well).

3. **Does my belief help me feel the way I want to feel?** If you are feeling an emotion you do not want to feel, the belief that's causing the feeling does not pass the third rational question. Consider how the belief makes you feel. Is it a positive emotion, or are you feeling an emotion you don't want to feel?

Let's look at our example above in terms of these three questions. We'll begin by looking at the beliefs:

You believe you are a failure who will never be able to do your job. Is this based upon objective fact? How could it be? If you were indeed a failure, you would have been fired a long time ago. You do not fail at every task, do you? Does this kind of thinking help you achieve your short or long-term goals? If your goal includes advancing at your job, this type of thinking is a hindrance. After all, "failed" employees seldom achieve success at any job. Does this belief help you feel the way you want to feel? Not unless you like to exist in the depths of depression, it doesn't.

You will soon be fired, and to lose your job would be unbearable. Is the first part of this true? Did your supervisor give you a warning that you were close to the axe? If not, what makes you think the belief is valid and true? Would it really be unbearable to lose your job? Every single day many people lose jobs and they go on to search for another one. Perhaps you have even been let go before. You "bore" it, didn't you? You found this job; you will find another. Looking at this belief in terms of your goals, if you need to improve your skills to advance, how much motivation to do that will you have if you "believe" that you will be let go? These kinds of beliefs are counter-productive, and will only increase your anxiety levels.

By disputing these irrational beliefs, the *D* of the REBT model, we arrive at *E,* which represents the new set of consequences or outcomes based upon the rational beliefs we put in place of the irrational beliefs. Now, our *ABCDE* model looks like this:

A. Your employer calls you into her office and criticizes you for messing up an assignment.

B. You believe you are a failure who will never be able to do your job, and/or you will soon be fired, and to lose your job would be unbearable.

C. You feel depressed, sorry for yourself and extremely
    anxious. When you leave work, you stop at the bar
    on the way home....

D. You are NOT a failure; if you were, she would have
    simply let you go. Of course you can properly
    complete the assignment; you just need to work a
    little harder or smarter. If you believe you will soon
    lose your job, you will not be motivated to improve
    your performance, and being fired could become a
    self-fulfilling prophecy. Even if you were to lose this
    job, you could find another.

E. You feel a little down, but you understand what you
    did wrong and tell yourself you will try harder on the
    next assignment. You are grateful your supervisor
    knows you are capable of doing your job.

We all think irrationally at times, and correcting this is
an ongoing project. We will never eliminate the tendency to
think that way, but we can reduce the frequency, the
duration, and the intensity of our irrational beliefs. First we
have to realize we do not just *get* upset, we upset ourselves by
holding and nurturing inflexible, irrational beliefs. We cling
to them because they represent the familiar, but the only way
to eliminate the unhealthy feelings is to work hard at
changing our beliefs.

Each time we notice an irrational belief, dispute it, and
change the associated feelings and behaviors, we create a new
neural network, or strengthen an existing one. With
continued practice, this new network will eventually
supersede the old, so that the same activating event will evoke

healthy beliefs and positive outcomes.

Let's look at a different kind of activating event, one that's a little more subtle. This one focuses upon drinking, but the principles are the same regardless of the addictive behavior. Instead of emotional upset, these beliefs lead to an unfortunate course of action. The scene is a national sales meeting, one of many I attended over the years. The night before, I drank too much, stayed out way too late, and was pretty wasted for most of the session. Now it is the end of the day, and I'm making plans for the evening. I don't want to get hammered again because I have to make a big presentation the next morning to the entire group. I agree to join the other salespeople at the hotel bar, so we can discuss where to have dinner.

A. The sales meeting is over for the day

B. I must meet the other salespeople at the bar. If I'm not sociable, they won't like me. I worked hard all day; I deserve it. I can get to bed early and be ready for tomorrow.

C. Felt I could control it, and that tonight wouldn't be like last night.

Of course, the night turned out just like all other nights, on the road or off—with me closing a bar, stumbling to bed, and being nonfunctional most of the next day. (That is a good example of the insanity of using—doing the same things repeatedly, expecting different results.)

The beliefs above were the same lies I told myself for years, and yet still thought they had some credibility. To start with, where is it written that I *have* to meet the other salespeople at the bar? Is it a job requirement? Will they stop liking me if I don't drink with them; where's the evidence for that? In fact, where is it written that I even have to go to dinner with them? As far as I know, I have never had just one drink in my entire life unless I was in a position where I couldn't get any more. I always believed "this time it will be different; this time I will control it." For 26 years I told myself that lie, and for 26 years I believed it. In all my time on the road I don't think I ever once went back to my room after dinner—not once! Yet, when I told myself the lie, I believed it.

I continued to be on the road for a length of time after I quit drinking, facing many of the same situations. More than once, especially in the early days of sobriety, I had to consciously dispute my well-honed, irrational belief system, and it went something like this:

D. The belief that I can have "only one" is false, and a prime example of magical thinking. Where is the evidence that this time will be any different than any other time I tried to have only one? Is there any evidence that this particular night will turn out different from every other night I spent on the road? Do any of these beliefs help me reach my goal, which is to be alert and functional in the morning?

E. Realized I couldn't control it, and knew tonight was going to be like last night because I was going to do the same thing as last night—not drink.

After a time, using REBT to change our beliefs becomes

nearly automatic—if we pay attention to the thoughts going through our heads. I'll give you an example. One night during the holiday season, I was staying in a hotel I had stayed in many times before. In order to reach the dining room I had to walk past the bar, decorated for the season and full of men and women enjoying themselves. The people were gathered in knots of two or three, chatting back and forth, smiling and laughing. Christmas music was playing softly, and a fireplace at one end of the room bathed the entire scene in a soft, friendly glow. I wanted badly to join them, just for a little while, to enjoy a brief bit of companionship in the middle of what had been a fruitless, lonely trip. I even took a step into the room; that's how much it affected me. This was the kind of gathering I could never pass up when I was drinking.

Before I took a second step into the room, I turned away, chuckling softly to myself. *Yeah, right,* I thought, *just a couple of drinks! Forget you never in your life had just a couple; forget once you have a drink at the bar, chances are you will end up having your dinner there, and closing the joint. Forget about "companionship." Nobody will talk to you after you have a few drinks, except other drunks, and then you'll end up telling (and listening to) the same stories repeatedly. Forget about the appointment you have in the morning; you will be too hung over to make it.*

Those are new thought patterns, new ways of perceiving old familiar situations and events. They evolved by applying critical thinking skills to irrational beliefs and disputing them. After a little practice it becomes second nature, and forgoing addictive behavior becomes your new habit, replacing the old. The more we practice the new behavior, the stronger the new neural networks become.

This has been a brief introduction into the REBT method. In subsequent chapters, we will learn to apply these principles and tools in managing specific situations and emotional upsets.

Language, and why it's important

The language we use often indicates the irrationality of our beliefs. When we use words or expressions like must, should, have to, need, can't, always, can't stand it, never, I'm a failure, and other similar words or phrases, we set ourselves up for feelings of despair, depression, and anxiety. We often find that merely changing the words we use is enough to allow us to see the activating event in a different perspective.

The expressions above are absolute, meaning they convey certainties, in a world where nothing is certain. Consider this statement: "I *must* not fail at this task or I am *worthless.*"

What does that imply? Does it really mean anything? Does failing at a single task make you worthless? Of course not, but we use that kind of language all the time.

What if we substituted the word "prefer" for the word "must" in that statement, and changed the rest to read, "*I prefer not to fail at this task because I want to do it correctly.*" Does that make more sense? Will that fill you with anxiety like the original phrase? The difference between the worst case being having to do the project over, or being a complete failure, is vast, and makes all the difference in the way you feel about yourself, doesn't it?

How about this statement: "I *need* to get that promotion;

if Jim gets it, I *won't be able to stand it.*" What does that mean? Sure, you *want* the promotion, but do you *need* it? Need implies something you cannot live without, like air or water. Is the promotion in that category? Of course not. It's okay to want something, people wanting things keeps the world moving, but need? Using the word *need* puts a whole new level of stress on the situation that's not called for.

Let's look at the second part of the statement above. What does "*won't be able to stand it*" really mean? Does it mean that if you do not get the promotion you will leave the company? That might be a true statement, but that decision opens a completely new can of worms, doesn't it? Does it mean your ego would not survive having to face the other people in the company if you do not get the promotion? Does making that statement further your goals? Not if you want to advance in the company. Does the statement add to your stress? Does it make you feel the way you want to feel?

The language we use to describe situations and events can be either helpful or harmful; language can either add to our stress load or detract from it. What if we changed the entire statement to, "*I want that promotion, and I won't like it if Jim gets it instead of me.*" See the difference? Which statement more accurately reflects the real world, does the most to further your goals, is the less stressful?

We are all under enough stress just living with others, without purposely adding to it by our choice of language. Here are some common words we use, and alternates that are less stressful and more reflective of reality:

Must	Prefer
Should	Desirable

Have to	Choose to
Need	Want
Can't	Choose not to
Never	Rarely
All	Many or some
Always	Often or frequently
Can't stand	Don't like
Awful	Bad behavior
I'm a failure	I failed at…

Those are just a few; I bet you could add a lot more if you thought about it.

Self-worth is not a variable

Even more important to our emotional health than the language we use to describe everyday situations are the terms we use to characterize the most important person in our lives—ourselves. Every single day we use words like jerk, dope, fool, moron, and even worse to define ourselves. Sometimes we use language like this in our heads, and sometimes say it under our breath or even aloud as though we have sentenced ourselves to ongoing perpetual judgment. We create a no-win situation resulting in our going through the day with self-worth rising and falling in relation to how we think our "ideal" self should function. We rate our individual attributes and arbitrary traits, none of which could ever define our intrinsic self-worth, and yet we behave as though they do.

Do you think green is good or bad? You might say

something is more or less green, or that green is bad for some purposes, or even that you don't *like* green. What you cannot honestly say is that green is *intrinsically* good or bad. Similarly, we cannot accurately and honestly rate *ourselves,* our *essence* as good or bad. We do, though, and cause ourselves great emotional disturbance by doing it.

Do yourself a favor. Refuse to rate yourself. When you catch yourself doing it, chuckle, and correct the internal language to reflect the true situation more accurately. Instead of thinking (or saying): *"What did you do that for, you dumb jerk!"* Try: *"Next time, try to focus more on what you're doing."* The first remark makes a general statement about your whole persona, while the second merely acknowledges that perhaps you weren't "there" as much as you should have been.

This concept is part of what we call Unconditional Self-Acceptance, or USA, and you will see it referenced in the upcoming chapters. What we shoot for in USA is a complete acceptance of ourselves for no other reason than that we are alive, and we have the capacity to enjoy our existence. We have various traits, and we behave differently depending upon our experiences and how we perceive the situation.

The important thing to remember is *we are not our behavior.* We can assess our behavior, along with our various traits, but what we cannot honestly do is evaluate something as diverse and complex as our entire selves. We have many traits, and we cannot judge our entire selves based upon any one of them. If we do, we invariably end up causing ourselves emotional upset as a result.

No one else can give us self-acceptance, it can only come from ourselves. The best part is that we are free to choose it at any time.

Chapter 9: Into Action

Urges and neuroplasticity

Let us consider where urges come from, and how they develop. In Chapter 3, I introduced a simplified version of the reward learning process, explaining how we record an entire pleasurable experience so we can repeat it in the future. We store cues and triggers, along with everything else that is relevant to the experience of using.

We are all familiar with the experience of walking into a home where a holiday meal is cooking. The smells and the warm, friendly environment combine to start our gastric juices flowing as we contemplate the pleasure of the coming meal. We cannot help it. We start munching on whatever might be available, even though we know a heavy meal is coming.

Many of the triggers that act to perpetuate our addictions work in the same way. Something as subtle as the tinkle of ice in a glass can bring about an urge to drink, seemingly out of nowhere. This is our limbic system noticing these cues and trying, with the aid of our well-formed neural networks, to recreate the pleasurable experiences we had while using. If we listen, we can hear the justifications coming from the so-called "thinking" parts of our brains, those voices in our heads that give us so much trouble.

Sometimes the smallest cue can trigger a particularly strong memory. For example, for several years after I quit drinking, the smell of a wood fire coupled with the sound of quiet conversation in a restaurant setting would produce a vivid memory of an evening I spent at a ski lodge in Vermont during a sales meeting.

Big flakes of snow were falling lightly outside, as we sat in the dining room, warmed by a roaring fireplace and several excellent bottles of wine. The food was wonderful, the conversation electric, and the mood festive. When I recalled the experience, I remembered that part, conveniently forgetting what happened later. I drank for several hours, finally tried ice-skating on a frozen pond, falling and injuring myself.

These environmental cues are always about times or events when we had fun. They concern experiences that involve others, usually warm, convivial times, before using deprived us of most normal human interaction. We recall the good times because they encoded as rewarding experiences; we do not recall the bad times, or at least they do not become urges. The sight of someone throwing up in a public restroom has never given me the urge to drink, although I had that experience myself upon more than one occasion.

The best technique for dealing with this type of urge is to think it through. What happened later, what is the rest of the story? How did these types of experiences turn out in the later stages of your using? Face it, you are not trying to change your behavior because you were having too much fun.

Another kind of urge derives from our using habits. I'm talking about arriving home at a certain time, and opening a beer or pouring a drink. Getting into the car or answering the phone and lighting a cigarette; going out for a "few" after work with your friends. The "Saturday night" syndrome, if that was your night to party. These are "muscle memory" urges. Deeply ingrained ruts in our neural pathways, well-honed by years of traffic.

You can avoid some of these urges by changing the underlying habit, like not stopping at the bar after work, others you just have to endure. The rest of this chapter discusses effective techniques for dealing with them.

Emotional upsets triggered by our established belief systems produce the toughest urges to resist. One of the things using has taught us over the years is that we *should not* have to suffer any emotional discomfort, for any reason whatsoever. Whenever we became aware of discomfort, we medicated ourselves so as not to feel it.

The strongest urge I had after I stopped drinking occurred just before we left our house to go to a friend's house for dinner. I remember a vague feeling of anxiety that came out of nowhere, and slowly built up to the point where I really wanted a drink, just to sooth my nerves. At the time, I had no idea where the anxiety was coming from, or what to do about it. The anxiety—and the urge—dissipated as soon as we arrived at our friend's house. Thinking about it later, I realized that for 26 years I seldom faced any social occasion without first addressing my feelings of anxiety with a drink (or two).

Occasional discomfort and anxiety is a natural part of life, and we as ex addicts have to learn to deal with it. That learning process begins with looking at that part of our belief systems which tells us that we shouldn't have to experience those feelings in the first place.

Many of the urges we experience are due to the learned portion of addiction, the part that is easiest for us to address. If we can learn these cues and triggers, we can replace them over time, but only if we realize what they are, where they come from, and how to address them.

Urge FAQ

As most of you probably know, FAQ stands for Frequently Asked Questions. There are many myths about urges, and I hope I will answer your questions here. If not, the appendix lists many sources to which you can refer for more information.

Before I get started with the questions, I want to say a word about why quitting alcohol is different from quitting most other drugs or behaviors. If you are a heavy drinker, you might consider checking yourself into a detox center when you first stop because you could do yourself serious harm. Statistics say the mortality rate among heavy drinkers who quit cold turkey is somewhere between one and three percent. I probably should have checked myself in because when I quit I was up all night as the ghost of every lobster I ever murdered came out of the walls after me. I never ate boiled lobster again.

The following are questions that you may or may not have on your mind about urges to use:

Are urges to use normal?

Any substance or behavior that is addictive becomes associated with behavioral cues or triggers that can bring on powerful urges to engage in the behaviors. There is no addictive behavior that I am aware of that is immune from urges. The strength and frequency of the urges varies with the individual and the substance or behavior, but they are always present to some degree.

Is it possible to resist them?

Yes. If it were not possible, there would be no recovered addicts, and 75% of us wouldn't recover on our own, or with minimal help.

How long do they last?

That depends upon the substance or behavior, but most last ten to fifteen minutes or less. The duration and frequency of urges declines as the person gets further away from their last use.

Do they follow a pattern?

Typically, an urge will begin at a low level, rise to a peak, and then decline until the addict is no longer aware of it. If we dispute the urge when it is at a low level, it lessens the peak of the urge.

Are they caused by something, or do they just appear?

The cause can be an outside event that has triggered using in the past, a thought, a chance run-in with a drinking friend, almost anything. They can also just come seemingly out of nowhere.

Can I avoid them?

Not really, but you can avoid your known using triggers. If you have a favorite bar, do not drive past it on your way home. If you have a favorite drinking friend, do not go out after work with him or her into situations where you used to use. This is a common sense thing.

Will they ever go away?

The further you get from your last using experience, the less likely you will be to experience strong urges. I have not had a drink since 1990, and I cannot honestly remember the last time I had an urge to drink. What I get now are thoughts, like, "Wouldn't a nice bottle of chardonnay be great with this dinner?" I chuckle and forget it almost as soon as it comes into my head. Drinking is not something I do now, so I instantly dismiss those thoughts. Actually, my urges to drink were never that strong anyway. Smoking urges were quite strong for two months or so, and then tapered off to nearly nothing. It varies with the individual and the substance or behavior.

Do they get harder to resist if you give in?

I cannot answer that question personally for drinking because I only quit the one time. What the research says is that giving in increases the duration, strength, and frequency of your urges. The first time you try to quit any addictive behavior is the easiest, no question. Makes sense, if you look at it from the standpoint of disputing irrational thinking. Each time you relapse, it's more difficult to tell yourself that you will have bad consequences if you do not have any.

Strategies to cope with urges

In the last section, I mentioned that urges were normal. Also normal are the cravings we feel for the effects of the substance or the behavior. Cravings are the "I want it badly" feelings that precede urges, and act as cues for them. If you can accept cravings and urges by realizing that you can choose not to engage in the behavior, you understand coping.

When urges first begin, they can seem almost impossible to resist. Our bodies are screaming for the effects of the drug, our anxiety levels rise, the voice is shouting in our ears, and even our minds seem to betray us with all of the justifications it comes up with for using. Most relapses occur in the first thirty days of any change process when the urges to use are the strongest. It follows that preparing to cope with urges is the most important thing we can do early on to set ourselves up for success.

An urge does not begin at maximum intensity, it follows a wave pattern, and you might not be aware of it at first or realize what it is. Perhaps you are having a busy day at work, and you hardly notice as your anxiety level begins to rise. It's getting closer and closer to five, and you would expect your discomfort to begin easing as your day is almost over, but it inexplicably continues to rise. Getting into your car, a thought drifts through your head that *a drink or two would sure quell this ache in my gut.*

You begin the drive home, and your anxiety level is still rising, *where the hell is that coming from?* You wonder. You start thinking about the bar near your office where you used to stop with a few of your friends after work. *Gee, if I turn down this street, it's right there, and I can see the guys and have a coke.* Your anxiety level goes a little higher at that, and you start feeling that you have to stop at the bar or you will never make it home. *It won't hurt just this once; I'll just stop and say hello; I don't have to drink.*

Once inside the bar all of the triggers that successfully kept you drinking for so many years surround you. You might get away with drinking Coke…this time and perhaps the next as well, but eventually, if you keep coming, you will revert to your old patterns. Each time you walk on the edge and get away with it, it becomes that much more difficult to resist the urge to engage in the old habit.

The further along we let the urge take us, the harder it will be to eventually resist it. How much more effective would it have been in the example above if our hero had made a firm resolve when he first noticed his rising anxiety level? He did not start out to harm himself; all he wanted to do is address his own discomfort and he did it in the only way he knew.

What if he had focused upon something he wanted to accomplish that evening, instead of focusing upon the discomfort? If he were prepared for the urge, he would have noticed it sooner and been ready with a coping mechanism.

The three most popular strategies for coping with urges are:

- Escape
- Avoidance
- Distraction

We can leave and remove ourselves from the urge-provoking situation. The classic example of this strategy is a party at a friend's house or any other get-together situation that normally provokes urges. You do not have to turn yourself into a social recluse, but what you can do is get to the party late and leave early, especially if you feel the urge to use while you are there. Contrary to your belief, no one at the party will notice.

Avoidance would be not going to the party in the first place, and if you think it would bother you that much, perhaps you should not go this time. Practice the habit of recognizing in advance the situations that would expose you to using triggers. An example is a sales meeting I had to attend, in another city, when I was less than thirty days sober. A friend suggested that I consider staying in another hotel, thereby removing the temptation to meet the other salespeople after the sessions and go out to dinner. I did it, and nobody even noticed I wasn't there.

Distraction is what I suggested in an earlier example. Change the focus from the urge onto an activity. Of course, we must have other things to do before this tactic is of any real use. The best things are activities that you enjoyed before using got the best of you. For me, it was reading and woodworking, but I'm sure you have your own hobbies and activities. Anything that requires your complete attention is fine.

You can count things, you can meditate, you can play word games, carry a Sudoku book around with you, anything that will take your mind off the urge. It will be gone soon of its own accord.

Think the urge and the using behavior through to its conclusion. Using has consequences, which you identified in your CBA. Keep them in the forefront of your mind as the urge runs its course. Consider where the first drink leads, and the possible consequences. Write down your "benefits of stopping," and keep the list in your wallet or purse so it's handy when the need arises.

One strategy that many people use is an *urge log*. Keep a record in a notebook of what time you first notice the urge, how strong it was on a scale of one to ten, and when you notice that it's gone. In addition, keep track of what you think might have brought it on, if anything. Sometimes, we know, sometimes we don't. If you know what brought it on, you can use the log to identify situations that are high-risk for you. Over time, you will notice that the urges will become weaker, shorter, and less frequent.

The language we use to describe urges and the manner in which we view them has a lot to do with how much discomfort we feel because of them. If we cling to the irrational belief that "we shouldn't have to tolerate discomfort," or, even more strongly, "we must not feel discomfort," we are really making the problem worse, not better. We can use the REBT technique described in the last chapter as a means to change these irrational beliefs.

If A is the urge itself, the B is the irrational belief we associate with the urge. Sometimes it's the belief that we "can't stand" the urge, that it will eventually overcome us, so we might as well give in now and avoid the discomfort. It might be that "the urge will get stronger, and we can't resist it." Whatever the belief is, it certainly is not helpful, does not make us feel the way we want to feel, and is not true.

As with any other cognitive method, it is not enough to read the words, or even to believe them. To modify your thinking, you must consciously dispute the irrational thoughts every time they appear. If you do this often enough you will create new neuronal pathways, and the urges will not be as strong, or last as long. Eventually the same stimuli, the tinkling ice cubes, etc., will not generate urges at all.

Cultivating mindfulness

As time goes on, more and more studies are indicating that mindfulness is an important part of recovery. Even in 12-step, mindfulness plays a role in the correct interpretation of step 10. In the cognitive therapies, mindfulness is an important component.

How do we go about 'cultivating' mindfulness? Do we have to begin a formal Zen practice? Must we become a Buddhist, and if so, what particular sect? Should we resign our present religion, if any, give away all our possessions, and go into a monastery? Fortunately, the answer to all those questions is a resounding no!

Mindfulness is nothing other than *being there,* present to our lives, and in the moment. What does it mean to be "in the moment?" it means nothing more than chopping wood when you are chopping wood, washing dishes when you are washing dishes, and talking with a friend when you are talking with a friend. It means that when you are doing those things, you are doing those things, and you are not mentally "somewhere else."

I mentioned in Chapter 3 how mindfulness could enhance learning. In the last chapter, I introduced cognitive techniques that require you to pay attention to what is going on in your own head. You should be aware of what you are thinking, and how you are responding to events in the real world. How will it be possible for you to dispute irrational beliefs if you are not aware of them in the first place?

Does this mean that you must be constantly aware and focused on the present in order to recover? I do not believe there is a human being on the planet who can say they are present to their lives and in the moment all of the time. Our brains just do not work that way. What we can do, with a little bit of effort, is train our minds not to wander quite so much, at least when we're trying to focus on the present.

There are several means of doing this, but I am only going to present one, the one that I have found is the simplest and the most easily accomplished. It is a modification of a Zen technique I have used for many years. For those of you familiar with 12-step, this exact technique was presented in an article in the "Grapevine" many years ago, and was included in a Grapevine audio tape, so it's conference-approved. Take what you need and leave the rest.

The technique is quite straightforward, and requires no special equipment or knowledge. All you need is a relatively quiet place, a chair or couch, and your mind. I have done what I am about to describe while driving a semi, sitting in an airline terminal, and in my own living room. When you first start, I suggest you seek out a place where you will not be disturbed for a few minutes, where you can sit comfortably, and that is as quiet as possible.

It does not matter what you sit in (or on). It can be a favorite chair or a couch, with or without arms. It only matters that you are comfortable. This is not an endurance test; it's a practice designed to help you focus your mind.

Sit comfortably, with your back as straight as possible. You can fold your hands in your lap, dangle them, leave them on the arms of the chair, or anywhere that's comfortable. I find that folding them in my lap works best for me, but you are free to experiment. Close your eyes or focus them on a spot in front of you.

Focus your attention for a moment on your feet. Let them relax; make sure they are in a comfortable position. Move up to your knees and do the same thing. Feel all of your body parts relax and get comfortable. When you get to your head, move it from side to side slowly, let it go forward and back, and feel the muscles in your neck relax.

Breathe in and out normally. Observe your breathing. Notice your chest expanding and contracting as the breath comes and goes. Listen to the sounds in your nose, throat, and chest. Feel your whole body relax.

Start counting your breaths. In and out equals "one." Count to ten, then go back to one again and start over. Keep counting. Thoughts will intrude, and your mind will drift. If it's a busy day for you and you have a lot going on, many thoughts will intrude and take you away from the breath. This is normal.

When you realize you are not focused upon your breath,

acknowledge the thought, and bring yourself gently back to the count. Start over with one. Bring yourself gently back; do not admonish yourself in any way for drifting off the count. This will happen many times when you are first starting to meditate; it is completely normal. Be gentle with yourself. That is one of the most important parts of this exercise.

Sensations will also take you away from the count. You might feel cold, a body part might start to tingle, or a fly might land on your arm. Acknowledge it, but do not go with it. Bring yourself gently back to the breath.

What do I mean by acknowledge the thoughts and sensory inputs? They are valid thoughts and inputs. You don't want to discourage or ignore them, just notice their presence, acknowledge that they're real, and gently put them away, saving them for later. When they return and take you from the breath, as they will, put them away again.

The object here is nothing more than to begin training your mind to focus in a particular manner. There is no goal other than that. You probably will not become enlightened, move to a higher plane, became a guru, or start a cult. What it will do, besides completely relax you for a time, is make it easier for you to stay focused upon what's going on in your own life. It might surprise you, when you start noticing how your thought patterns jump around, seemingly at random. Meditation will also, over time, make it easier for you to "quell the disturbance" when you are in the middle of an emotional upset.

How long should you do this at each sitting? Good question, and the answer depends upon you. When you are first starting, five minutes will be plenty. Even if you only make it three minutes, you will start getting in the habit. The trick is to keep at it, even if it's hard and seemingly unrewarding at first. Keep at it. After you start seeing a difference, keep at it. Just keep at it.

Dealing with that voice in your head

Some people tell me that if they could get it down to only one voice, they wouldn't be concerned, but the problem is really the committee that meets up there at the drop of a hat. I agree, sometimes it sounds like a committee meeting instead of a single voice:

> *"Tonight won't be like last night."*
> *"Go on, you can have just one."*
> *"Give it to me I gotta have it!"*
> *"If I don't get this, I'll die!"*
> *"You deserve it."*
> *"I need it!"*

On and on, so it goes, and sometimes it seems like it never gives us any peace. Self-talk such as this is the harbinger of urges. It usually starts with a subtle message, which grows in immediacy and intensity until either we give in to it or the urge passes. One of the most important parts of controlling urges is dealing with this voice, and that is why this particular set of tools has its own section.

The first thing you have to realize is that we all have these voices in our heads, even non-addicts. They are like those old cartoons with the little devil sitting on one shoulder, and the little angel sitting on the other, feeding us conflicting opinions about which course of action we should follow. The addictive voices differ, however, in that they emanate from the limbic system, and therefore come at us with a stridency matched only by the messages concerning sex, food, and survival. Sometimes they are even stronger.

This voice is your mortal enemy, and the first thing I am going to suggest is that you give it a name. Yes, that's right, just like the imaginary friend you may have had as a child, only this voice is real, and dangerous. You can call it anything you like; I only suggest that the name you give it should reflect the way in which it appears to you. Some call it "The Enemy," or "The Terrorist." Whatever name you decide upon, it should be personally meaningful.

Once you name it, you can literally tell it to go to hell. Remember, it is a part of you that is trying to kill you—nothing less. A voice that tells you that you can get away with using "just once" is not trying to do you any favors, is it? Telling you that you "need it" is just plain wrong; you know better.

You might not even notice the first messages; they hide in your daily activities. A friend at work asks you to join him, and a few others, down at the corner bar after work, as you always do.

"Yeah," says the voice, "we can do that, and we can drink coke."

As the afternoon wears on, the voice gets a little stronger.

"C'mon, you know you always enjoy that, what's wrong with you, what kind of man are you that you'd let your friends down like that?"

And then, finally, "Look, jerk, there's no good reason we can't go and be with our friends, it's Friday, for goodness sake, and you deserve a break. You've worked hard all week. What are you worried about, you can just have one, you don't HAVE to get drunk."

So it goes.

The voice will fade, along with the urge. They will both ride off into the sunset together, as long as you remember that neither one has any real power over you, except for the power you choose to give it.

Some common pitfalls

Not everyone who tries to quit an addictive behavior succeeds on his or her first try; in fact, those who do are in the minority. There are things we can do to improve our odds of success, and most of these are just common sense.

The number one cause of relapse is stress. We cannot eliminate all the causes of stress from our lives, nor should we, as a moderate amount of stress is psychologically healthy. What we can do is learn to manage it better, and avoid unnecessary stress. Exercise, mindfulness techniques, improving your ability to rest, and better managing your time are a few ways to reduce stress. Learning to take better care of yourself in general is another. Some of us developed our addictions as a way of coping with stress, most of which was a result of choices that we made ourselves. Consider making different, healthier choices.

It seems almost unnecessary to suggest that you should avoid situations, places, and people who were connected with your addictions. It is surprising how many people in recovery think they can go on with their lives as before without making any changes. If you hang out with your drinking or using friends, you are extremely likely to use again. If you insist upon frequenting your old hangouts, chances are that before too long you will end up back where you started.

Do not let yourself get roped into old behaviors by

thinking you somehow have a duty to your old "friends." They'll get along just fine without you, and in fact will hardly miss you at all. About a year after I quit, I ran into an old drinking buddy on the street only to have him ask me where I'd been for the last "couple of weeks." When I tried to tell him he hadn't seen me in over a year, he didn't believe it.

The most important thing you can do when you are just starting to make a major change is to stay aware of your situation, your surroundings, your thoughts, and your beliefs. If we are unaware, we can slip into situations that make it very hard not to use, when a little foresight and planning could have made things a lot easier for us. Look for "out of the box" solutions to old problem situations; try changing how you think about things.

catching a bit at the end.

I looked around the room, and no one else had anything to offer. The board looked like this so far:

A. Didn't get promotion.

B. They had no right. They can't do this to me. Could lose my job. This kind of thing always happens to me, and will always happen. I will never get anywhere. I'm not worth it

C. Anger, fear, depression, wanted to drink

I wrote the letter "D" on the board, below the "Cs," and turned first to Jim. "Okay, Jim, the first two we can take together. First, are they true, would they pass the camera test? Do they have the right to choose the person they promote?"

"Yes," he answered, "of course they do."

"Ah, welcome back, rational Jim. Okay, do they make you feel the way you want to feel?"

"No, they make me feel angry, and like a victim."

"How about helping you meet your goals?"

"No, they don't help there either."

"Is there any actual evidence that you are going to be fired because they didn't promote you? Did they warn you?"

"No," he said, "I can see that is an irrational belief."

"The next two are basically the same, in that they both use absolutes like *always* and *never*. That's not really the case, is it?"

"No. This would have been my second promotion since I've worked there. In spite of the time I got drunk last month and missed a couple of days, they have treated me pretty well."

"Are you 'worth it,' Jim? Are you a worthwhile human

being? Are you worth the effort you're putting into your program and yourself?"

"Yes, of course I am, but why can't I see all that when I'm in the middle of it?"

"You didn't see it because disputing your beliefs hasn't become 'muscle memory' yet. Your mind is still following the old pathways, but you didn't give in, you didn't drink, and that's important. What have you learned from this experience, what can you take away from it?"

While Jim pondered the question, I wrote the disputes we discussed on the board, and wrote an "E" for the new consequences.

"I guess that I can get through this kind of thing without drinking, in spite of what my mind tries to tell me. From what I can see on the board, every single one of my beliefs was irrational."

"How do you feel now?"

"Relieved, mostly. They thought Stan would do a better job for them, and maybe they were right. Instead of feeling pissed off, I just want to go back and try to do a little better."

"So, the new consequences are that you're perhaps annoyed, but not in a rage, and you feel motivated to improve. No depression, or fear, is that right?"

"Yeah, that's right, but how can I do this when I'm in the middle of it? I can't stop and do REBT all the time. How can I avoid being so upset?"

"Good question," I said, "anyone have an answer?"

Ryan spoke up. He had been coming almost a year, and was doing well with his addiction to prescription drugs, and problems with anger management. "Hey, I know how you feel, Jim, it was really hard for me in the beginning. I would fly off the handle, and go from zero to rage in a heartbeat. All it would take is some jerk cutting me off on the highway, and I would get so upset I'd find myself pounding on the steering wheel. What I've learned here, though, is to never chase them past my exit."

That got a laugh from the group, and even Jim joined in.

"Seriously, I took it personally whenever something like that happened, and I just couldn't bring myself to do ABCs on the spot. I wasn't rational enough to see past the anger, so I learned a few simple tricks that made a big difference. The first one was what I call levitation."

I could see the newer members looking around, wondering what Ryan was talking about. He didn't leave them guessing for long. "I wondered what I would look like if I could see myself in the middle of one of my rages, so one day I imagined that I was floating above the highway and could see into all of the cars. There I was, pounding the steering wheel, while the guy I was so mad about was cruising along without a care in the world. I looked like a spoiled kid in a crib, just whining away, thinking the whole world was out to get him.

"The scene was so ridiculous, I couldn't help but laugh. Here I was, letting that guy live rent-free in my head, while he had no idea of what was going on behind him. He didn't know I was mad, and what's more, he didn't even care. I was going through life feeling that other people were doing things *to me,* when in actuality, they just *do them,* usually for reasons of their own, that have nothing to do with me.

"Another trick I use is to first tell myself that it's okay to feel annoyed or disappointed, but that I don't have to work myself into a rage even if someone really treats me badly. I make mistakes, and so do other people. If I get upset, I need to realize that whatever the problem is, it's never *too* upsetting, and I *can* stand it. Does that make sense?"

Jim admitted that it did, and we moved on with the meeting.

***

Self-defeating beliefs

Although it's fun to illustrate methods in a simulated meeting environment, it would take too much room to cover all of the possible irrational beliefs in that manner. In fact, it would be impossible to cover all of the irrational beliefs we can come up with in *any* manner, at least in a way that would fit into this book. Chapter 8 introduced many of the more common irrational beliefs, and highlighted the language we learned to describe ourselves and the rest of the world. Here I am going to describe some of the more common self-defeating beliefs, along with the ways we can dispute them.

You may notice two things as you are going through the list. These irrational beliefs are not new; they are variations on the same theme as others we have explored, and most of them affect our self-esteem. The messages we send to ourselves are far worse than any we receive from the outside world. These are in no particular order.

"I should always feel happy, confident, and in control of my emotions, I should never feel angry, anxious, inadequate, jealous, or vulnerable."

First, notice the absolutes, *"should always,"* and *"should never."* Anytime we start thinking in absolutes we are asking for trouble. Emotional upsets are difficult enough to resolve without beating ourselves over being in that position in the first place. Whatever they are, our feelings are indeed valid, and a result of our current belief system, healthy or not. Being upset for being upset makes no logical sense, and keeps us from looking at the underlying belief that caused the upset.

"I must never fail or make a mistake because people will not love and accept me if I do."

They say about addicts that we are people with huge egos and low self-esteem. We never seem to meet our own ridiculously high standards, and we set ourselves up for failure time and time again. Most of us are walking contradictions when we are using, and these beliefs take a long time to root out. When I first stopped drinking, I continued treating people the same way as I did before, and it took me a while to figure out why.

For many years, I never let anyone see the twisted ugliness I kept hidden inside myself. I knew I would be banished if anyone ever saw the real me. The only way I could face myself was if I was successful in dragging those around me down into the slime with me. I had to bring you down to my level, and I did it by verbally assaulting *your* self-esteem.

When we first stop using, many of us compare our twisted ugly insides to the smooth and serene outsides of those around us. What we do not understand is that most of us feel the same way about ourselves when we first quit. We've all done things, said things, and thought things that we aren't too proud of; we are, none of us, unique. As we work on our own self-esteem, we soon find it no longer necessary to build ourselves up at the expense of others. We find that as we practice Universal Self-Acceptance others accept us as well.

"My worth as a human being depends upon my achievements, or my intelligence, or my status."

In Chapter 8, we discussed self-worth as a variable. We found that we could not rate ourselves as people based upon one or two arbitrary traits. If we do, our self-esteem will rise and fall with our subjective view of each day's achievements—and failures. We have intrinsic value as human beings, and one of the most valuable lessons we can learn is to treat ourselves as our own best friend.

"I am responsible for everybody and everything."

We see ourselves as all-powerful sometimes, and yet the only things we really control are our own feelings, beliefs, and actions. Once we realize we are not responsible for others, we usually feel a tremendous relief now that the weight is off our shoulders. We are now free to focus upon the things we can control, and one of those is our own recovery.

"My needs are not important, and I should not spend time taking care of myself."

Of all the self-defeating beliefs, this one can be the most harmful because it goes to the heart of the messages we send ourselves. Every time we ignore our own needs, we are telling ourselves that we are worthless—others are worth much more than we are. Whether we mean it or not that is the message, and our addiction is only too willing to listen. The best way to dispute this belief is to start meeting your own needs first. If you don't know what they are, sit down and make a list.

What do you need? What would you change if you wanted to treat yourself better? Eat some good healthy food;

treat yourself to a meal out. Get plenty of rest and exercise. Do something you enjoy; see someone you like spending time with. Write that letter that has been on your to-do list waiting for a free moment. In short, try being your own best friend for a change instead of your worst enemy.

At times we ignore our own needs and do not even notice that we are doing it. We begin doing something we want to do, and the doorbell or the telephone rings. Off we go, serving the needs of a friend or loved one, and once again ignoring our own. Even the airlines tell us to put our own oxygen masks on first, before we help another. That's a valuable lesson we could apply in all the areas of our life.

"As soon as (_____) happens, I will be happy."

Fill in the blank however you like. It could be a new house or car; it could be a new job or lover. It doesn't matter what it is. We begin to recover when we realize that nothing stands between happiness and ourselves other than...ourselves. Happiness is something we choose, not something granted by an outside source. There is an old Zen saying that is appropriate here:

> *"I have lost my favorite teacup.*
> *I have two choices.*
> *I can have lost my favorite teacup and be miserable,*
> *I can have lost my favorite teacup and be all right.*
> *Either way, the teacup is gone."*

Most of the time events are out of our control; what we do control is our reaction to them. Choose happiness.

These are just a few of the self-defeating beliefs we use to beat ourselves up on a daily basis. To discover more of them, take a piece of paper and list your own personal self-defeating beliefs. We all have a few that we've clung to for years. They may have originally come from others, parents, teachers, etc., but they are now part of who we are. Much of the process of recovery is ferreting them out, disputing them, and sending them on their way.

Managing stress

There is an old joke in AA that has been floating around for many years about the alcoholic's often overblown reaction to stress. It goes like this, "If a 'normal' person (non-addict) has a flat tire, they call the Auto Club; if an alcoholic has a flat tire, they call the suicide prevention hotline." This implies that an addict is not only more sensitive to stressful situations, but that they also focus on the stressor and blow it out of all proportion.

I know when I was drinking it seemed to me that stress was all around and caused by nearly everything and everyone with whom I came in contact. Part of the reason I drank was to relieve stress. When I began to research addiction, one of the primary questions I wanted to answer was whether addicts are indeed more susceptible to stress, or was the old AA story just unfounded folk wisdom.

Studies show that recovering addicts do display a heightened stress response as compared with social drinkers. The response manifests itself both in physiological signs (heart rate, blood pressure), and in brain responses in areas known to be associated with cravings and urges.[51] Obviously, the more cravings and urges the addict experiences, the more likely they are to relapse, so learning to manage stress is an important part of recovery. Not only is managing stress important, studies show that *how* we manage it may be just as important. Those who avoid problems that need addressing rather than working through them are more likely to relapse.[52] To succeed we have to learn to live in reality; we can neither alter nor avoid it.

In the eighth century an Indian Buddhist scholar, Shantideva of Nalanda University, wrote the following lines:

> *"If there's a remedy when trouble strikes,*
> *What reason is there for dejection?*
> *And if there is no help for it,*
> *What use is there in being glum?"*

That is the earliest known precursor to the "Serenity Prayer" that leads off most AA meetings and is not a bad way to begin a discussion on ways to manage stress and interact with reality. There are two types of stressors: those situations where we can make changes that alter the situation itself and those where we cannot alter the situation and must make changes in how we view it. In either case, many strategies are available to us.

I would like to start by making a distinction between avoiding problems that need addressing, and avoiding stressors while going about our normal activities. When we are trying to recover, one of the first things we learn is that we can run but we can't hide, at least not from ourselves. There are things that give us that "tight feeling," like a knot in our gut, whenever we think of them.

- We owe money to our friend that we cannot repay right now, so we avoid our friend, hoping we don't run into them, instead of calling them and explaining the situation. The longer we delay, the tighter the knot gets, and the more upset we become.

- Our apartment has a leaky faucet, and instead of contacting the owner we delay because we are afraid he will think we are chronic complainers. The drip gets worse, and finally we lay awake at night listening to it with a tight knot in our belly from anger and frustration.

- We procrastinate on an assignment at work and avoid our boss, who we're sure will reprimand us for being late. As the knot tightens, we even start blaming the boss, even though it's not her fault.

- We are overwhelmed because our significant other isn't performing their fair share of the necessary tasks. Rather than have the needed confrontation, we bury our feelings and tell ourselves it's best to just "soldier on." As the knot tightens and the anger grows, we resent the other person for not figuring out what is going on with us.

In situations like these, avoiding necessary actions increases rather than decreases stress. The study referenced above proved that addicts who deal with stress by avoiding it experience twice the number of cravings in a stressful day compared with those who use problem-solving strategies to understand and deal with the stress. Most of the time, when we confront problems rather than ignore them, they turn out to be nowhere near as bad as they play out in our heads.

In the rest of this section, we will look at two types of situations:

- Those where we can change the situation by either

avoiding or altering the stressor, and

- Those where we cannot change the stressor, so must adapt.

Change what we can

Much of the stress we feel is self-inflicted. We want to please people, and we want to get through life with the least amount of hassle and pain. In the early stages of recovery we come face to face with the things we have done in the past, and we feel guilty about some of them. These feelings tend to make us reluctant to confront those around us, so we find ourselves taking on more tasks than we can handle.

The first thing we can learn is how to say "no," sometimes one of the hardest words in the language to say. We want to help; we want to "be there;" but the cost is much too high if it leads to eventual stress. We need to know our limits, and stop thinking that we can do everything. Consider analyzing your "to-do" list, and distinguishing between the things you should do and those you must do. Drop tasks that aren't necessary down to the bottom of the list, or eliminate them.

We can learn to manage our time better. When we take on too much and run behind, it's hard to stay calm and focused. Try to plan, and don't overextend yourself.

Sometimes people in our lives stress us out. We can work to turn the relationship around by being a little more assertive, if we are willing to compromise. After all, if we ask someone else to change their behavior we must be willing to do the same ourselves. If we are willing to bend, just a little, we may find a happy middle ground.

We can take control of our environment, and limit the

amount of stress in our lives. If watching the evening news bothers us, we can stop watching it. If discussing certain topics, like politics or religion, with our friends stresses us out, we can avoid such discussions. We don't *have* to be right. It's much more beneficial to us in the long run to be calm and composed.

Accept what we cannot

Many situations we cannot change, but remember: our *perceptions* of events, not the events themselves, upset us. Sometimes all we have control over is what goes on in our own heads, but usually that is enough. There's no way we can prevent or change stressors like the death of a loved one, a serious illness, or the loss of a job. In cases like that, we have to work towards accepting things as they are even though it may be difficult.

One useful tool is to look at the big picture. Put the stressor in perspective, and try to see how much it will matter in a month or a year. My wife had a friend who used to say: "How much does that matter in the cosmic scheme of things," whenever she came to her with a new problem. When we do this, we find many problems just aren't worth our getting upset.

Sometimes we can reframe the problem. What appears to be a stressful situation from one view can turn into something entirely different from a new angle. Being stuck in a traffic jam, for instance, can become an opportunity to do some work, listen to your favorite radio station, or just spend time alone.

Try to keep the focus upon the positive things in your life when events of the moment start getting you down.

Instead of dwelling in the negative, reflect upon your own qualities and gifts. Most reasonable people would agree that no matter what is happening now, more things are going well in their lives than going badly. Keep things in perspective.

The behavior of other people is out of our control—always. People do things for all sorts of reasons, most of them having nothing to do with us. Keep this in mind when someone's behavior creates a stressful experience for you. We live in an imperfect world, and people make mistakes. Do not harbor anger and resentments. If someone is living rent-free in your head, you can evict them without notice and feel an immediate relief.

We are not islands. Talking through a stressful situation with a friend or loved one can be a great relief, even if nothing you can do will change the situation. Just having your feelings validated can make a world of difference.

In 1999, I had a near-fatal heart attack that was partially due to the stress I was under trying to run my own business and pay the bills. I remember lying in intensive care believing that my life was over, and I would never be able to do anything worthwhile again. Both of those beliefs turned out to be wrong, but one thing I had to do was learn to manage stress.

My first important stress management tool was exercise. I worked up to four miles a day on the treadmill, and did other exercises. I started utilizing most of the tools in this section, some suggested by friends and family, and others I adopted because they just seemed to make sense. A year later, I was driving an 18-wheeler for a national trucking company. It was the fastest way to making a reasonable amount of money, although it was hard on the body.

I never read as much in an equal period as I did during the two years I drove a truck. Of course, it was books on tape, sometimes as many as five or six a week. I studied all kinds of subjects, everything from history and philosophy to art and music. It was a wonderful education, and one I would have missed if I hadn't nearly died and then been willing to drive a truck for a living.

Professional driving is a very frustrating occupation, with a lot of hurry up and wait, and many things that are out of the driver's control. I learned a great deal about myself during this time, especially how to keep an even temperament.

I am a firm believer in the theory that whatever doesn't kill us makes us stronger. I survived that heart attack, and instead of finding myself at the end of the road, it turned into the beginning of a wonderful life. Fourteen years later, I'm living at 5,000 feet in a small village in central Mexico, surrounded by a thriving expat community. I play softball twice a week, walk everywhere, volunteer at our local library, and facilitate a local SMART Recovery® group that I started. In short, I survived to do whatever I want to do because I learned to manage everyday stress in my life.

Wisdom to know the difference

It is not always clear whether or not we can change a particular situation, and if we should even if we can. Many situations are obvious; the few remaining cases offer the most opportunity for upset. We like to think we can change almost anything, but that is not the reality.

We need look no further than our own recent history to see how short the list of things we can change really is. How many times have you tried to control the behavior of other people? How did that work out for you? The hardest lesson for me was learning that I was a lot better off after I set my sights on being happy rather than being right. How many arguments have you ever won? (I don't mean in your own eyes.) How many times did the other person stop arguing, recognize that you were right, and change their opinion?

Yes, it does happen, but very rarely. Most of the time arguments continue long past the point where it becomes clear that neither person is going to win. Our own experience tells us (or should) that in the end *we* are the losers. We pay the price in emotional upset, and the price is always too high. The best way to handle emotional upsets is not to have them in the first place. Avoiding senseless arguments, and even the people we tend to have them with, is an excellent way to start.

How many of our emotional upsets are due to our efforts to change either the past or the future? We agonize over decisions we made that we can no longer revisit and allow people to live rent-free in our heads long after the real or imagined offenses occurred. We hold "he said, she said" conversations between a future adversary and ourselves in an attempt to mold the future to our wants and perceived needs. All these things come at the expense of enjoying the moment.

As we get further into a healthy recovery we begin to realize that all we have is the moment. Not only is it all that is important, it is all that we can influence—what is happening right now, in this moment. The conversation we are having with a friend, a stolen moment with a loved one, an interlude with a child or grandchild. We give these up, all the time, to waste our precious moments on vain attempts to change the past or influence the future. There is peace and serenity in the moment; everything else is an illusion.

Chapter 11: Learning From Relapse

Using is always a choice

"Well, I found myself at this party, and everybody else was drinking, so I figured what the hell, I might as well drink too."

"I had a fight with my wife and she really got to me, so I left the house, went to the bar, and got drunk. You would too if you lived with her."

"Oh, I don't know...I was out to dinner with a couple of girlfriends, and they ordered a glass of wine so I did too. I did it without thinking; it was just habit."

"My boss reamed me out over a mistake I made and it really upset me, so on the way home I drove through a neighborhood where I knew I could get what I needed."

"I was just walking down the street, and suddenly I was struck drunk."

The last one is a joke, but it's not much different from those above, is it? After a period of abstinence, using is always a choice—always. It never happens by accident, and never without an opportunity for conscious thought. We have cues and triggers that sometimes produce cravings and urges, but no matter how strong they are, we can resist them.

Often the best opportunity to overcome the urge is when we make the decision to put ourselves "in harm's way." We decide to go to parties, we let people get to us, we let situations overwhelm us, and we blow things out of proportion. What it boils down to, many times, is that we want to use more than we want to not use. We learn that using (for us) *is* the easier softer way, and we are not quite convinced we want to stop.

There are also those who are very well motivated to stop using, and they relapse anyway. If motivation is the "key to recovery," why is it some of us who are convinced we cannot use safely, and want to quit, still have problems with relapse? Is relapse an unavoidable stage in the change process, or are there things we can be aware of that lessen the possibility?

Estimates are that 90% of those who recover from addictive behavior experience at least one relapse along the way. This chapter will increase the odds in your favor by presenting common warning signs and behaviors that precede relapse, along with examining the underlying beliefs. Remember, we must modify the beliefs to change the behavior, not the reverse.

Relapse warning signs

In 1982, two researchers, Terence T. Gorski, and Marlene Miller, identified a set of warning signs that typically lead to relapse. [53] Further research has validated these changes in attitudes and behaviors, and proven they are accurate predictors. As you read this list, realize these changes occur gradually. Recognizing them early in the cycle will allow you to see beneath the behaviors, and modify the beliefs that drive them.

- Change in attitude — Something isn't quite right. You're doing fine, but you notice recovery is not as important to you as it once was. You are drifting, and something is wrong, but you cannot identify a good reason for it. You are unsure of yourself, and your ability to overcome your addictive behavior.

- Elevated stress — It seems you have many problems

in your life, and your stress level is rising. You tend to overreact to the stress or act impulsively. Watch carefully for mood swings and exaggerated positive or negative feelings.

- <u>Denial</u> — Not a recurrence of your old denial of addictive problems, this is a denial of the elevated levels of stress you are feeling. You do not manage the stress well because you are denying it in the first place. What is worse, you dismiss your worries and don't talk about them with others. Denial of reality is always dangerous for addicts, especially in early recovery.

- <u>Recurrence of withdrawal symptoms</u> — Anxiety, depression, sleeplessness, and memory loss don't necessarily stop a few days after we quit. Sometimes they can continue for months, and other times they disappear for a while only to reoccur in times of stress. These symptoms add to the stress we are already feeling, and of course, the danger is that we could decide to self-medicate these feelings with our drug of choice. Sometimes we make these feelings even worse by telling ourselves we "have been sober long enough that we shouldn't be feeling like this." This could lead directly to a feeling of "what's the use, why am I bothering?"

- <u>Behavior change</u> — When you quit, you probably made changes in your daily routine to make it easier to replace your compulsive behaviors. Now you start deviating from your healthy routine and drifting back into your old behaviors. Instead of honestly evaluating your behavior, you either avoid or become defensive when someone calls it to your attention. You may begin to use poor judgment and act without thinking things through.

- <u>Social breakdown</u> — You begin to feel uncomfortable around others, and you find yourself making excuses not to socialize. You stop hanging around with non-using friends, and you may withdraw from supportive family members. If support meetings are part of your program, you cut down the meetings or stop going altogether. You begin to isolate yourself. You may experience the fear of being found out and banished.

- <u>Loss of structure</u> — You begin to abandon the changes you made in your daily routine. You may sleep late, ignore personal hygiene, and stop eating regularly. The plans you do make do not work out, so you overreact and stop making constructive plans. You may focus on one small part of your life to the exclusion of everything else, and you may feel listless and depressed.

- <u>Loss of judgment</u> — you have trouble making decisions, and the ones you do make are unhealthy. You have difficulty managing your feelings and emotions. You stop using *ABCs*, or any other method of changing your beliefs. Perhaps it's hard to think clearly, and you confuse easily. You feel overwhelmed, and you anger easily. It may be hard for you to relax.

- <u>Loss of control</u> — You make irrational choices, and

are unable to interrupt or alter those choices. You actively cut off or avoid people who can help you. You begin to think you can return to and control your drug use. "This time will be different!" You lose confidence in your ability to manage your life, and you may begin to believe there is no hope.

- Loss of options — You stop attending all meetings, including those on-line and with therapists; and may stop taking any prescribed therapeutic drugs. You feel helpless and desperate. Feelings of loneliness, frustration, anger, resentment, and tension overwhelm you. You might start thinking how foolish you were to believe you could beat your addiction, and you cannot imagine life without the drug.

- Relapse — You try "controlled" drug use and are disappointed in the results. You feel shame and guilt, and your drug use spirals out of control. Your problems with relationships, jobs, money, mental and physical health all come back, worse than before.

Not a pretty picture, but it's not destiny either. You can stop the progression at any point along the line by recognizing the symptoms and taking action.

A questionnaire, developed under a grant from the National Institute on Alcohol Abuse and Alcoholism, is extremely accurate in predicting relapse. Called AWARE, for Advance WArning of RelapsE, it consists of 28 questions you can score yourself. If you suspect you may be on the road, you might want to try it. If you do try it, pay careful attention to the scoring on the individual questions, as not all score the same. The questionnaire is available here. [54]

As important as it is to watch for the behavior changes above, it's just as important to correct them when we recognize them. That should go without saying, but unfortunately, experience has shown it cannot. We are people who have lived most of our lives in denial, both of our true situation and of reality itself. Perhaps when we decided to quit, we looked back on our lives and believed we were just ignorant of what addiction had done to us.

If we examine the situation honestly, we must admit that what kept us in the dark for so many years was really closer to *willful* ignorance. In other words, we had plenty of clues; we just chose to ignore them. I know a man who once had all the symptoms of a heart attack: pain in the chest, arms numb, profuse sweating, nausea, gray complexion, and weakness. Instead of calling an ambulance, he lingered at home for nearly six hours before he finally let his wife take him to the hospital. I know all about the power of denial.

The best defense against relapse is not to start down the road in the first place. If we continue to practice the tools we select on a daily basis, dealing with our irrational beliefs as soon as we recognize them, we will never slip into the type of thinking that begins the process. The more we practice the tools, the more ingrained the program becomes. We begin to think, believe, and act like recovered addicts.

Dealing with setbacks

Okay, it's not the end of the world, although it might seem like it right now. The important thing for you to do is pick yourself up, dust yourself off, and not use a relapse as an excuse to continue engaging in your addictive behavior.

Paraphrasing Thomas Edison, you haven't failed; you've just found another way to stop using that didn't work. Don't give up. Examine the process and establish where you deviated from your plan. Not the plan to relapse, that was successful; I mean your original plan, the one to quit using.

If you look at the incident closely, you will find that lurking underneath the surface behaviors that led to the slip are irrational beliefs that need addressing. Discovering them won't make them disappear, but at least you will know what you are facing. The irrational beliefs that drive relapse behaviors are typically the core beliefs we hold about ourselves, and they can be the most deeply rooted.

Earlier, I differentiated between two possible causes of relapse: those due to lack of motivation to change, and those caused by stress and situations. Yes, some relapses have their roots in motivational issues, but it seems that whenever anyone relapses the first thing they do is return to the CBA to see where they went wrong. This is not always the best course of action, and sometimes may be the worst thing we can do.

Remember what we are really fighting here, our own minds. In Chapter 5 of *Alcoholics Anonymous,* pages 58 & 59, Bill Wilson describes the "disease" of alcoholism as being "cunning, baffling, powerful," as though it were a separate entity and beyond your power to control, but it is not. We have learned to be addicts, and learned well, especially the justifications for continuing with our addictive behavior. We have cultivated scores of them, all neatly tucked away to be available at a moment's notice. They are in working or habit memory, available at once, without the intervention of our conscious mind.

So, how do we divert the steamroller before it rolls over

us? One way is being aware of our thought processes. The signs of relapse in the last section are quite specific, and if we are vigilant they will give us a good idea of where we are. However, we have to *pay attention* to the warning signs for them to be of any value. Paying attention does not mean noting them and moving on, it means noting them and looking for the beliefs that are driving the behaviors.

If someone experiences a "slip" in AA, they drag themselves to a meeting, where they hear they must return to step one and recommit to the fallacy that they are powerless over their disease. Examining that belief in terms of neuroplasticity, you can see how self-defeating it is. We are fighting well-developed neural pathways that have been justifying our addictive behavior for years. To recover, we take responsibility for disputing these pathways and creating new ones. The problem and the solution are both within our own heads, and within our control.

The learning component of addiction is not magical; the process is well known and well documented. Addiction is not a spiritual malady caused by our character defects, it results from the formation of neural networks supporting unhealthy belief systems that drive our destructive behaviors. We are familiar with the behaviors, but we sometimes have a difficult time confronting the beliefs. What are the beliefs that justify behaviors that can overcome even our basic survival instincts?

In the last chapter I talked about self-destructive beliefs, many of which have to do with our self-esteem. It is primarily these beliefs that drive destructive relapse behaviors. They are the strongest and most ingrained of all our beliefs, and the ones that can most easily overcome the will to survive. Why would you want to survive if you believe the world would be better without you?

It is helpful to do an *ABC* on a relapse, to try to see the beliefs that drove the feelings that drove the behaviors. *A* can be almost anything, an actual event, a feeling, or a perception. If we look down to the *Cs*, or consequences, we will find anxiety, depression, anger, fear, and a whole host of other negative emotions. The beliefs, the *Bs* are a bit more complicated.

I find three levels of *Bs* that people express when analyzing a slip. The top level is typically the justifications that come out of the "thinking" portions of our brains. They are the ones that were always enough to keep us using in the past, before we decided to quit. These top-level beliefs are things like:

- I thought I could get away with it

- Nobody will know

- I can have only one

- It won't be like it was before

Emotion drives the second level, and they usually come out with a little probing:

- I deserved it

- I had to have it

- I couldn't stand it

The third level is closest to the core, and the hardest to admit and dispute. This level of belief underlies all the rest and is really the driving force behind any relapse:

- What difference would it make

- Screw it

- I'm not worth it

The first two levels are the commonplace thoughts and beliefs addicts deal with all the time in early recovery. They are the same justifications that kept us in denial for years, and we know how to dispute them.

The last level is the bottom line for most addictive behavior. We do not feel we are worth it, and it makes no difference to the world if we use or not. That belief must be disputed and rooted out, in all of its forms and manifestations. It is why Universal Self-Acceptance, and the entire framework of cognitive behavioral therapy are so important to the addict. Realizing that we *are* worth it is the cornerstone of recovery.

It is not enough just to dispute this belief intellectually, although that must be part of the process. We must *show* ourselves every single day that we *are* worth it and it *does* make a difference whether we use or not. We show ourselves by *not treating ourselves as we would not have others treat us*. I know it sounds backwards, but we would never let our friends get away with treating us the way we treat ourselves, would we? Would we let our friends call us horrible names and bully us? Would we let them keep us from fulfilling our own needs until we met every single one of theirs? Would we allow others to keep us from exploring ourselves, and considering all of the positive opportunities available to us?

You bet you wouldn't. Then why do those things to yourself? Why do you let yourself get away with it? Every time you sell yourself short you send yourself a powerful message that you're not worth it. Every time you allow someone else's priority to supersede your own, you tell yourself you are not as important as the other person.

Of course, we do have responsibilities to others. There may be children, jobs, spouses, friends, and people in our lives to whom we have certain commitments. Fulfilling those commitments is one of the ways we build self-esteem. However, we should strive for a balance in our lives, a happy medium between our commitments to others and the very important one we have to ourselves.

Make an appointment with yourself. Schedule a time just for you. Do something you really enjoy. It does not matter what it is, it can be sitting on a park bench feeding pigeons if that suits you. It does not have to cost anything. In early sobriety, I took lunchtime walks by myself along the riverfront in Wilmington.

You can meditate during your time, or pick up the phone and call someone you've been meaning to call. You can shop for yourself, or perform a task you've been putting off. It doesn't matter what you do or don't do; you are telling yourself that you are an important human being who is worth spending time getting to know.

Consider that it took our entire lives, up to now, and the "help" of parents, teachers, and others to lower our self-esteem to this level. We will not repair it overnight. One day though, we may discover we have become the person we always knew we could be.

If we believe we are worth it, we will be motivated to change our destructive behavior. If we believe we are worth it, disputing the rest of our self-destructive belief system becomes easy. If we believe we are worth it we will find a way to recover.

Chapter 12: A Balanced Vision for You

Lifestyle balance

Lifestyle balance is more about priorities than anything else. We can either set them for ourselves, allow others to set them for us, or we can set them according to what we believe others in our life want from us. When we are using we operate in react mode most of the time. Using is our number one priority, and everything else moves into the background until it becomes necessary for us to take action. When you are getting survival messages from your limbic system, your child's school play is not a big deal at all. Not that we don't neglect ourselves while we are using because we do—often dangerously so. We focus almost exclusively on the short-term in every aspect of our lives. We don't worry about tomorrow, next week, or next year, unless there is an upcoming interruption in our drug supply that we need to be concerned about.

We also know we are less than stellar helpmates, friends, or co-workers, and we use that knowledge to beat ourselves, adding to our stress load and perpetuating the cycle. We are overwhelmed, and at some level we are aware of it, regardless of what we try to tell ourselves.

When we quit many of us realize that we do not have the slightest idea how to live like those around us. How do they do it? How do they plan things and actually carry them out? What's the big secret?

It turns out it's not much of a secret after all. It's just a matter of learning to take care of yourself, and finding a balance between short-term gratification and the achievement of long-term goals. There is another name for that process; it is also called 'growing up.' Many of us never really did, and it's about time we learned how.

This chapter is about growing up and becoming a useful member of society. Along the way you will learn many important survival skills that will help you maintain your recovery. It begins with learning how to take better care of yourself, getting enough sleep, exercise, and eating well.

Taking care of yourself

Addiction is a thief. It steals money, friends, family, jobs, and eventually everything that is important to us. Its most insidious theft, however, is one that we seldom recognize. It is the theft of our most precious commodity—time. We spent vast amounts of time indulging in our addiction, and even more thinking about it, planning it, and recovering from it.

I was a daily drinker whether I was at home or on the road. At home my typical day began about ten in the morning. By then my eyes were open enough and the headache had retreated enough for me to do some useful work. I might make a few phone calls, but nothing serious would get done until I made myself lunch, accompanied by a couple of beers. Following my afternoon nap, I would have coffee around three, just waiting until 4:30 when I could legitimately have my first strong drink of the day. I would then drink until 1 or 2 the next morning, stumble into bed, rinse and repeat.

If I was on the road it was okay to drink with lunch, as long as it was a vodka martini or something "light" like that. No scotch or rye during the day, that was for drunks. Wine or beer, of course, was fine anytime; that wasn't *really* drinking, was it? I seldom took clients out to dinner while on the road, although my expense reports always indicated I did. That way I could cover any amount of alcohol and not have to pay for it myself. In my last year of drinking, I scheduled entire weeklong trips that were nothing but binges in one city after another. I felt entitled, that I deserved this kind of life. After all, I had been on the road for 20 years, missed most of my kid's childhoods, and made a great deal of money for my employers.

A few days after I crashed and burned, I woke up clear-headed one morning realizing I had a day to fill and nothing with which to fill it. One thing most of the newly recovering seem to have plenty of is energy—that and a short attention span. When we stop using, we all contract attention deficit disorder, or something very much like it. We cannot seem to keep our mind on one particular thing for very long without jumping to something else, and that makes planning and learning how to live difficult.

It's like we want to catch up with everything we've missed over the last however many years it has been since we started using—and do it in a couple of weeks. Some of us become missionaries, wanting to "carry the message" about how good we feel to everyone we think has even the smallest chance of suffering from addiction. Suddenly all of the empathy and compassion we have kept well hidden for years comes flooding out, threatening to drown all those unfortunate enough to be in our immediate vicinity. In short, many of us go from obnoxious to irritating, and from frustrating to unbearable.

Our friends and relatives are happy we are no longer

using, but now they wish we would just...well...get a life! Easy for them to say, they've all had lives. Most of us never had one, and we have to learn this along with everything else. As addicts we lived a strange half-life, always constrained by the needs and effects of our drugs. We were fooled (by ourselves) into believing we were living full lives, but we were mistaken. Does what I described in the beginning of this section sound like a life to you? Of course it isn't. However, I accepted my life as normal, as we all do when we are using.

If you have a regular job, with regular hours, you have an advantage I did not have when I quit drinking: a structured environment. I will talk about overcoming that lack of structure in the next chapter, but for now I am going to assume you have a somewhat structured environment.

No matter what your addictive behavior was, it severely affected your non-work hours and your financial situation, for many different reasons. Now that you are not using any longer you are free of those constraints, but I caution you to be careful with what you choose to do with your new resources. Most of us neglect ourselves while we are using, and when we stop it is important that we start taking care of ourselves in at least three areas.

The first area is eating, the second is sleep, and the third is exercise. They are interrelated, of course, as you probably know. The most common complaint we mention to the doctor during our sporadic checkups is that we "feel tired all the time." We do not make the connection between the drugs and sleep, as we do not make connections between the drugs and anything else. Therefore, every time we see our physician they tell us to eat better and get more exercise in order to improve our sleep habits.

While we were using our brain was doing the best it could to adapt to the stimulation of the drugs. When we stop, our brains do not return to normal immediately. Instead, you may be sleeping even worse now then you did when you were using. There is no cure for this, except time, but we can help the situation by doing a couple of simple things.

Try to eat healthy foods on a regular schedule. Eating regularly is almost as important as what we eat. If you were a heavy drinker, you may crave sweets for a while. No, your liver does not metabolize alcohol into sugar; it is a bit more complicated than that. Moderate drinking will actually lower blood sugar levels because the liver cannot produce glucose while it is trying to get the alcohol out of the bloodstream. Seems that the liver treats alcohol as a poison, and drops everything else to deal with it immediately. Later on, as we drink more heavily, alcohol interferes with the action of insulin, which has the effect of raising blood sugar levels.

I became a Snickers addict when I quit drinking. I didn't know why, but I needed the sugar. It is no accident that most AA meetings feature cookies, cakes, or donuts. It is okay to give in to these cravings if you have them, at least for a while. The sweets might help you avoid cravings and urges to use. You can always lose the weight later, and your new exercise program should take care of the excess calories.

Speaking of exercise, how much did you do while you were using? In spite of your intentions, how much exercise did you really get? You are not hung over in the morning anymore; how about considering walking or even running before breakfast. If you are close to a gym, consider signing up for a morning swim or exercise program. You have to do something with the money you're not spending on your drug of choice, how about investing it in yourself?

Your exercise program will depend upon your general physical health of course, and that brings me to another point. I suggest that you see your family doctor as soon after you quit as you can manage it. Tell him or her what you are doing and why. Be honest about what you were using and how much. Ask them to suggest a diet and exercise program for you. I do not necessarily mean a "lose weight" diet, unless you need that, but most people don't know what constitutes a healthy diet. Before you head off in a direction of your own, you might consider getting a medical opinion.

A word of caution here. Things have changed since I quit drinking in 1990, and I suggest that you do what you can to avoid having the words: "drug addict," "alcoholic," or any other such connotations appended to your official medical record. If you have attended a formal treatment program, there isn't much you can do, but there are ways of communicating information to your doctor without affecting your future ability to obtain medical insurance or employment. If you have a long-term relationship with a family doctor, they know anyway, you don't have to make an announcement. Other practitioners only have to know that you are "sensitive" to certain substances. Don't let your new-found honesty impinge upon your future prospects.

For most of us, sleep problems resolve themselves after a short time, especially if we pay attention to proper eating and exercise. Some of us continue to experience problems after a few weeks, and if you are one of them perhaps you should ask your doctor for advice. There is no need for you to continue suffering from lack of sleep, and it makes other aspects of recovery difficult. I guess the message is, learn to think enough of yourself to begin taking care of …you.

Goal setting

I was a sales engineer throughout most of my career. Every year at the national sales meeting, we would go through the exercise of goal setting. I hated it, I guess because they made us do it. I worked for three companies during those years, and they all attached a great deal of significance to the process. They would start with the company forecast, break that down to regions, than individual salespeople, and give us all our quotas. We would then break our quota down to the number of sales calls necessary to obtain that level of business, based upon averages. We would take it all the way down to number of phone calls per day necessary to get the required number of appointments. You get the picture.

I hated goal setting because the company set the objectives. In this section we will start from scratch and define our own goals. Believe me, it is more fun.

What is a goal anyway? It is a general statement about a desired outcome with one or more specific objectives that define, in precise terms, what is to be accomplished within a designated period. Sounds like quite a mouthful, but we have done it informally our whole lives, and now we are just going to add some structure. Goals are multi-level. By that I mean that we look at them in several different time frames. We take a major goal and divide it into bite-sized pieces that we can manage within reasonable periods.

If done correctly, the goal setting process provides both long-term vision and short-term motivation. It helps you to focus and organize your time and resources, so you can make the most of your life. By setting sharp, clearly defined goals that you can measure, you will see your own progress. You will raise your self-esteem as you recognize your ability and competence in achieving the goals you have set.

The methods of goal setting have not changed much over the years, although in the mid-eighties I learned an acronym for goal setting that still exists. They taught us that to be meaningful, goals should be:

- Specific — goal objectives should address the five Ws: who, what, when, where, and why. The goal should state specifically what is to be done, and by what date. "Continue my education" is not a goal; "obtain an associate's degree in nursing by June of 2015," is.

- Measurable — how will you know when you have achieved the goal? "Get more exercise" is not a goal; "work up to walking four miles a day by June 1st" is.

- Achievable — a goal should be within your control and influence, and possible for you to accomplish. If you are forty years old and have never played ball, you probably won't ever pitch for the Yankees no matter how badly you might want to. (Unless you happen to be left-handed with a good cutter, of course)

- Relevant — a goal should be consistent with your system of values, and relate to them in some way. Establishing goals in an area of your life that is not important to you is just setting yourself up for failure.

- Time-bound — goals should have a specific, defined

target date for completion. In the absence of a target date they are not goals, they are wishes.

The acronym, of course, is S.M.A.R.T., but it has nothing to do with SMART Recovery®, although they use a variant of this acronym in their program.

Now that we understand what a goal is, we can begin to set some for ourselves. A good place to start is a determination of what is important to us as individuals. In other words, what are our values? In Chapter 5, we performed a simple exercise that should be enough to start pointing us in the right direction. If you have the worksheet from that exercise, look at it now. If not, make a list of the things that are important to you, in no particular order. From that list, pick the five that are the most important, again in no particular order.

The list could include such things as health, family, or career, for instance, or anything else you consider important. This is your list, not mine or anyone else's; there is no right or wrong. Once you decide what is most important to you, you are ready to begin the goal setting process. Start by picking a value, one in which you recognize the need for improvement, and think of a goal that would make sense.

Let us say one of your primary values was "career." You might be tempted to set a lifetime goal to "run a company and retire rich." That is a nice sentiment, but it's not a goal by the SMART definition, is it? What sort of business would it be? Do you have the necessary skills and resources? What do you consider "rich"? To turn that sentiment into a workable goal, or series of goals, you have to be more specific. Lifetime goals are fine, but to be measurable, we have to be able to condense them into smaller increments.

Try looking at the next five years, what would be a

reasonable goal in that period? Perhaps your goal might be a higher position than you have now, with either your current firm or another. What would be necessary in terms of skill, education, and experience to obtain that goal? What can you do to work towards your goal in the next year, what would be your incremental goal? Do the same for six-month, one-month, and one-week time periods.

At the one-week level, you can do a daily task list defining what you intend to do during the period to advance this goal. Do the same for the goals you will establish in the other four areas you picked in your values list. It all sounds very confusing, but it does not have to be. If you begin with your top five priorities, determine specific measurable goals, each with an overall time frame, it should be easy to break them down into achievable units.

At this point, it is time to start putting things on paper (or the computer, if you prefer). There are many different types of goal setting worksheets available on the web, and you can find them by doing a search. If you would prefer to make your own, it is easy enough to do; I have provided a model for you on the next two pages. You can also download this worksheet from powerlessnolonger.com.

Goal Worksheet

Category/Value: _____

Overall Goal: _____

Today's Date: _____ Target Date: _____

Start Date: _____ Date Achieved: _____

Specific: *What exactly will you accomplish?*

_____
_____

Measurable: *How will you know when you have reached this goal?*

_____
_____

Achievable: *Is achieving this goal realistic? Do you currently have the resources to achieve this goal? If not, how will you get them?*

_____
_____

Relevant: *Why is this goal significant to your life and values?*

_____
_____

Time-bound: *When will you achieve this goal?*

_____
_____

The benefits of achieving this goal will be:

_____
_____

Potential Obstacles   **Potential Solutions**

_____   _____

_____   _____

_____   _____

Who are the people you will ask to help you?

_____

_____

_____

_____

Specific Tasks: *What steps do you need to take to achieve your goal?*

Task	Target Date	Completed
_____	_____	_____
_____	_____	_____
_____	_____	_____

At the top of a sheet of paper, first write the category or value associated with this particular goal. On a line below, write the overall goal and the date by which you expect to achieve it. Next, go through the five points of the SMART goal system, listing how this goal meets each point. The next page starts with a statement of the benefits of achieving the goal, followed by the potential obstacles and their solutions. Who are the people you might ask to help you in achieving this goal? Write them down as a reminder to contact them. Finally, what are the specific tasks that you need to perform to achieve this goal, and when do you expect to complete them? It is important to make a note on the form when you complete each of these tasks. Seeing yourself making progress towards your goals is part of what provides the motivation to continue.

Once you finish making worksheets for all of your goals, you are ready to do the weekly list discussed above. Once the incremental tasks are "out there" where you can see them, they will be difficult to ignore. Successful people understand the importance of managing their time, as it is the only way to accomplish long-term goals. As you are checking things off from your to-do list you will be building self-esteem, the single most important factor in a successful recovery.

This process will not only show you that you can achieve your long-term goals, it will also make it possible for you to measure your progress on a weekly basis. It will turn what seems like an impossible task into a manageable series of simple steps. Many of us have dreamed dreams for years, but most of them never went beyond the person on the next barstool. We talked a lot but we never did anything about it.

Part of taking responsibility is learning to manage our own lives, knowing we are responsible for what we are becoming—and where we are going.

Journaling

In Chapter 4, I described an incident that happened before I quit drinking, involving an email to a friend. Responding to her concerns about my drinking, I typed the words "only every night and only to oblivion." This was the first time I realized the power of the written word. I stared at those words for a long time before I sent them on their way, and they haunted me for months afterward. They marked the end of the lies, if not the drinking. Because I had given them life they were "out there," and I could no longer deny that I was out of control. From then on, no matter how many lies I told myself, I knew in the back of my mind how every night would eventually end.

Several people in AA told me it was a "good idea" to start journaling, but when I asked them what that meant they gave me vague answers. I got the impression that they didn't do it themselves, and couldn't explain it to me. When I started seeing a psychiatrist, he told me the same thing, only his instructions were a little more explicit. He told me to start with daily events, like a diary, then move a little deeper into my thoughts and fears when I was comfortable.

His advice sounded fine, but I was feeling so good that I didn't think I needed all that malarkey. It was okay if other people couldn't keep track of their own thoughts, but I was sure that I could, so I didn't need that foolishness.

Before I quit drinking, I had registered to take a couple of courses at a local community college. I do not remember why I did that, but I do remember telling my wife that at least it would be two nights a week I didn't drink. Looking back, I am surprised I said that—especially while I was still drinking. One of the courses was a writing seminar, kind of a critique group, which started about three weeks after I quit.

When I wrote pieces for that group, many things came out that I did not expect. As I typed, the manuscript would start going in directions that I never planned. Later I learned that this is something that happens to all writers, even those who write self-help books.

While I was with that group, I wrote hundreds of words about…well…myself. Who I was, what I was doing, where I thought I might be going, how I was going to get there, who was going to help me, how I was feeling, and so on. The process was not only cathartic it helped me organize my thinking and was the beginning of my own personal road to recovery.

I began to carry a notebook around and write my thoughts down as they occurred to me. Writing by hand, with a pen, was more powerful than seeing the same words on a computer screen. I found that what I wrote was less important than the act of doing it, and the less thought I put into the writing the more compelling it became.

Almost none of what I penned in those first few months ever saw the light of day. I wrote for myself, not for others, mostly during the day when I was alone in the house. While I unraveled the twisted, evil thing inside myself, I was terrified of anyone seeing the writing. I destroyed the notebooks almost as fast as I filled them, and that, according to some, was a mistake. There might be something to gain by looking back and rediscovering the person who wrote that drivel, but he does not exist anymore, and good riddance.

I journaled for about nine months before I tapered off and stopped. At that point, nothing screamed to come out anymore, and what I wrote seemed forced and contrived. Over the years I have worked some things out through journaling, but I don't call it that anymore, I call it blogging. I do not mind if people see it because although they may disagree with me, I'm perfectly happy with who I am and don't mind defending my views. The computer went off on some real tangents while I was writing this book, but thanks to the editing process I will not inflict them upon you or anyone else.

I recommend journaling, and give it broad definition. You can begin anywhere you like, go anywhere you like, and do with it anything you like. I found words on paper, put there by ink or graphite, to be more compelling than the same words on a computer screen, but you may not. Try it both ways and see for yourself. It did not seem to matter when I wrote. First thing in the morning at home, after everyone left, worked just as well for me as a hotel room in another city before I went to bed. It was kind of like meditating; as long as I was alone and quiet it was okay.

If you buy a notebook or sit down in front of your computer and cannot think of a thing to write, don't worry about it. Start writing about your day so far, or even describe the room you are sitting in; it does not matter how you start. Once the words start appearing you will be surprised how they seem to take off in directions you never intended. When you find yourself looking at the paper or screen and wondering where the hell *that* came from, you will know you are doing it right.

One more word of advice—do not edit. Do not think about how your writing sounds, or about grammar and syntax. Just let the words flow as they will; do not censor them in any way. Falling into the trap of searching for the "right" word or phrase will stop the process cold. Do not worry about how your words might look to others; none but you may ever see them anyway. The important thing is to get them out there *where you can see them*—you are writing them for yourself.

Helping others

Helping others does not mean that we should turn ourselves into obnoxious born again missionaries. Personally, I do not want to see anyone suffer from addiction one moment longer than necessary. I do not care what they try to do to stop; I want to help them any way I can. At the same time, I realize that nothing will work until the addict *wants to quit*. Our main job is to not stand between them and a realization of their condition. We can also help to make them aware that they are capable of change, and we can be there when they decide they want to make that change.

We all know what an *enabler* is; in fact, you probably had one or more. From friends who bailed us out of jail to wives or husbands who hid our using from the kids and our employers, we have all had little helpers. If we hadn't we never would have been able to use as long as we did. When I was doing my drinking, police officers were still in the mode of letting people drive home with nothing more than a warning not to drive drunk again. Were they doing me a favor? No, I do not think they were.

Have you ever lent a car to a friend who lost his license

because of a DUI that "wasn't his or her fault"? Do you think you were doing them a favor? Few people get only one DUI; most get several before the legal bills pile up and they can no longer ignore them. What was their liability has now become yours. Are you willing to bet your house and your future that they will not have an accident in your car, under the influence, and injure someone? Let them walk, take a bus, or call a cab. They will have more time to consider their position, and you will sleep better.

Assuming that you have read this book up to this point, you understand more about addiction than you did when you started. Perhaps you can see instances in your own life when people did you "favors" that, considering subsequent events, were not favors at all. Keep this in mind when you are contemplating helping someone.

This can be especially difficult when the suspected addict is a family member or a significant other. Our inclination is to always give them the benefit of the doubt, and believe they are sincere when they swear that if you help them this time they will never do it again. The truth, as you very well know, is that they *will* do it again, and at the very next opportunity. If you need counsel from an outside party, get it—then take their advice, no matter how hard it may seem to you. In these situations, professionals, and those who have been through it before, can see the problems, and the solutions, much more clearly than you can.

If you are a recovering addict, your story is more powerful than you might think it is. As I was writing this book, I tried to put as much of my own story in it as I could, and there was a reason for that. If I could not prove to you that I have been where you are, why in the world would you listen to me? I would be just another person who did a little research and thinks he has a way out. The way out is based on the evidence, but unless I had some experience with it I would not have much credibility, would I?

The night I first stumbled into AA I saw plenty of sufferers, yes, but I also saw people with clear eyes and a spring in their step. When I realized they had been where I was, I wanted what they had, and I wanted it right now. It turns out that there is a lot more to recovery than clear eyes and a spring, but noticing those was enough to get me started and keep me interested. Do not hesitate to share your story and your feelings with others. Even if they don't "see it" now, your experience may be another chink in the wall of denial that surrounds all of us.

We never know what effect our words might have upon others. When the realization of my condition hit me, it was not a single event. It was the culmination of many separate and distinct bits of information, gathered over the years from many different sources. Many of those sources were people who had been where I was. It took a while for me to realize that where I was, was where they had been.

It is a rare and wonderful thing to be there when someone reaches out for help. I cannot imagine a thing I would rather do than help someone in the initial phases of recovery. It can be rewarding, but it can also be extremely frustrating, especially if we forget that *we are not responsible* for their recovery. We cannot overcome their addiction; only they can do that. If you are going to meetings, take them along if they want to come, and step aside if they decide to take a path other than yours. Remember that there are as many paths to recovery as people who have successfully recovered, and you do not have the only ticket. You can show them what has worked for you, and leave it up to them to take what they want and leave the rest.

Why work with others? When I was new in AA, I would make "twelfth-step" calls with a friend in the slums of Hartford, Connecticut. Several times a month we would pick up drunks and take them to detox. I gave people rides to meetings and back, spent endless hours trying to convince them not to drink, and cleaned up after them when they did. I was always on call, and almost never refused to go out when the phone rang. I did that for a couple of years, and I can honestly say that as far as I know, I never got anyone sober. However, every single one of those calls was successful because *I* stayed sober.

I am not suggesting you do any of those things; I do not even know if people do them anymore. What I am suggesting is that you consider making yourself available to others, either directly, on the phone, or over the internet. SMART has meetings on their website, so does AA. You can be as anonymous as you wish. I encourage you to work with others, at least in the beginning. Support, especially from others in the same situation, is very important in the early stages. Even later on, you will find it beneficial to continue to do what you can to help others. Remember that you will be helping yourself at the same time.

Chapter 13: Thoughts on Recovery

First

When I was writing Chapter 12 two of the sections started writing themselves, straying from my outline into territory that was not part of my plan. *Powerless* originally included only those methods and programs that had an abundance of evidentiary support. However, several things that were important in my own recovery, and many of those I have observed, do not fit easily into any of the prior chapters.

That is what Chapter 13 is about—everything else. Things I have learned from experience that you may not find in studies, surveys, or other self-help books. Little here is unique to me; most of these are ideas and suggestions I owe to others.

As you move along the path you will find yourself adapting and making your own, ideas that at least on the surface, have little to do with recovery. You will adapt them because they resonate; they make sense to you and appeal to your understanding of "rightness." These are mine. They are not necessarily yours. That is for you to decide.

Reduce stress

When I decided I no longer wished to live as I was living before, the prospect frightened me a great deal. Not only was I going to have to learn ways of coping with the same stressors as other people, I had to learn to live as they do, and get along with them as well.

Sometimes our lives are upset when we first decide to

quit. We go off in all directions, unsure of what to do next. Early sobriety can be like hitting the brakes on a car going 60 on ice—lots of spinning around and bumping into things before you come to a stop. Often our stress load increases when we begin to face the real world without our drugs, and we have few tools with which to deal with it.

That was certainly true in my case. My first two years were very traumatic, not only for me but for most of those around me. A first marriage ended, a second began, and I was living in a different state with my daughter and my new wife. (Yes, my daughter forgave me for the poem and we have a good relationship today, thanks for asking.) I started a computer repair and networking business, and for a few years, things were stable. I was working in a high-stress environment, but I was coping pretty well—or so I thought.

A major heart attack in 1999 changed everything once again. I had to sell my business, quit smoking, and eliminate as much stress from my life as I could. The suggestions below were not ones I adapted overnight, or acquired from any single source. They are a distillation of ideas that resonated with me, taken from many different people and places, beginning with my first months of sobriety and continuing up to the present time. I cannot cite any studies that show these principles are effective in overcoming addiction, but perhaps they can give you some ideas you can use to reduce stress in your own life.

The principles are these:

- Give yourself permission
- Live in the moment
- End your own suffering

- Try to live your life so as to increase the sum total of joy in the world, while decreasing the sum total of misery.

Give yourself permission

We thought we were free when we were using, but we were not. The servicing of our addictions restricted our options to only those that would perpetuate the addictions, leaving us unable to make simple choices now, when we are free to make them. When we were children, we learned to ask our parents' permission to do things. As we grew older, we began to give ourselves permission to do things.

The time has come to start giving ourselves permission again, this time to do things that lead to healthy beliefs and behaviors. A good place to begin is by giving ourselves permission *to be good to ourselves.* Think about it. We have a 10-foot internal bullwhip, and for years we have been using it on ourselves. Why do we do that? We do it because our belief system tells us that we deserve no better. We can turn that around by treating ourselves better, but first we have to give ourselves permission to do it.

Do you remember the story of the teacup from Chapter 10? All that stands between us and being happy is giving ourselves the *permission to be happy.* We can choose to be happy even if the world is falling down around us, if we just give ourselves permission. That does not mean that we are ignoring what is going on, it just means that we have chosen not to allow ourselves to be drawn into depression, anger, fear, or other negative emotions. Those negative emotions are paralyzing, while a calm, confident demeanor is a great platform for problem solving.

We can give ourselves permission to *plan for the future,* now that it looks like we may have one after all. In the depths of addiction, the future seems to get closer all the time, doesn't it? We start out planning for our retirement, but by the time we are ready to quit using we can think no farther ahead then the next high or the next drink. Now we can begin making plans again, and working for the achievement of long-term goals.

It is important for us to give ourselves permission *to do the things we need to do to maintain our recovery.* If we do not do that, the rest of the permissions do not make much sense. By giving ourselves permission to do these things, we are reaffirming that we are worth the effort, and that we can prevail.

Along with being good to ourselves, we can give ourselves permission *to do things we have always wanted to do,* now that we have the time and the available resources to do them. One day, about a month sober, I spotted a beautiful pair of cowboy boots in a leather shop. I had always wanted a pair, ever since I was a kid, and they were about the price of three days' supply of the scotch I used to drink, so I bought them. They pinched my feet, and I could not wear them two days in a row, but I never regretted buying them. Every time I wear them I remember what they represent.

Live in the moment

The tools and techniques in *Powerless* work best if our focus remains in the moment. We cannot observe or influence our thoughts and beliefs if we are not "there" to notice them in the first place. Can we do this all the time? Of course not, but we can teach ourselves to bring our focus back to the moment when we notice that the stresses of the day are getting to us.

Consider this. Right now, in this moment, you have everything you need. You are sitting comfortably somewhere reading a book, and perhaps trying to understand what I am talking about. You may be in the middle of a stressful day or at the end of one, but right now you are calm, focused, and in the moment. In the next moment your mind may drift, bringing thoughts that could disturb your tranquility, but right now you are here with me. In this moment *you are equal to your life,* are you not?

Yes, you have cares, worries, fears, and other things that pull you from the moment, but they all concern things that *may* happen, don't they? They aren't right here right now, are they? As we pass through life we deal with it one moment after another, whether we focus upon it or not—that is just the way time works. We have no choice in the matter. We are either there or we are not, *life happens anyway!*

Have you ever observed children playing, either by themselves or in a group? They focus upon what they are doing, and are oblivious to whatever may be happening around them. That is because children are completely in the moment, like puppies, without a single care about the future. Just a few years later, we take them out of the moment, sometimes forever. Do you remember how slowly time passed when you were a child? Summer seemed to last forever for you, while for your parents it passed in a heartbeat. You were in the moment then, and your parents were not. With school off in the distant future somewhere, with no cares or responsibilities, you were able to wring everything possible out of each and every moment.

I am not trying to convince you to renege on all of your commitments and obligations. I am talking about living *in* the moment, not *for* the moment; there is a difference. If you have a decision to make in this moment, make it. If there is something you need to think about in this moment, do so, and then put it aside. Chop wood when you are chopping wood, wash dishes when you are washing dishes, and make plans when you are making plans.

Two major offenders in preventing us from staying in the moment are worrying about the future and rehashing the past. If you are like the majority, most of the things you spent your valuable moments worrying about never happened. Even when the things you worried about happened, did worrying make the least bit of difference? Of course not. We believe that if we worry about something happening, it is the same as doing something about it, and it isn't. If worrying about the future is a waste of time, rehashing the past is even more so. Reflect, learn, and move on.

This moment, right now, is all you have, and it will never come again. If you let something take you out of it, you have squandered it. There is peace and serenity here, in this moment.

End your own suffering

These four words encapsulate the entire theme of *Powerless No Longer*. They are also the central message of Zen Buddhism, but I am not trying to make Buddhists out of you. Recovery from any addiction is a difficult process, and we can make it more so if we fail to keep the focus upon ourselves. We are the object of the exercise. This is *our* life we are talking about, no one else's. We cannot beat our addictions if we are doing it for anyone other than ourselves. This effort is about us, completely and absolutely—that is the only way it will work. The research proves it.

In addition to keeping the focus upon ourselves, we must remember that we are responsible for all of our own suffering. Suffering is as much a choice as relapsing, and we have just as much control over it. Emotional pain is inevitable. It becomes suffering only if we choose to allow it, instead of choosing to use the tools found in *Powerless*.

Our thoughts and ideas about the way things *should* be versus the way they are causes our personal suffering. Suffering is the difference between our expectations and reality. Changing our beliefs about events, and the way the world should be, is the way to end our suffering.

Try to live your life so as to increase the sum total of joy in the world while decreasing the sum total of misery

I do not want to get preachy here, and I am not trying to make you into a saint, honest. What I am suggesting is that you consider this along with your other moral and ethical guidelines. Let me explain. Everyone comes to recovery with a different background and set of experiences. Some of us have a rigid moral framework based upon our idea of how the world should work, while others have adapted a situational morality that works for them.

This is not to say that either of these is good or bad, I'm asking you to consider that if morals and ethics were based upon how we treat one another on a daily basis, instead of an arbitrary set of rules that categorize human beings according to individual traits, would that not provide a less stressful environment? If we were to lay aside our prejudices, preconceived notions, and our need to be right or better-than until we can get our feet on the ground, do you think we would have an easier time in recovery?

I am not for a minute suggesting you leave your church, quit your religion, or change your worldview. Often how we perceive and subsequently treat others can either raise or lower our level of stress, and that is what's important to people in recovery.

Unless you are a sociopath, you know the difference between right and wrong. You always have. You know when you are bringing another person joy, and when you bring pain. Yes, there are instances when we inadvertently cause pain to another, but that is not what I am talking about here. I am talking about seeing our fellow human beings as just that, nothing more or less. Seeing the world that way reduces ethics and morals to simply trying to do the next right thing, in this moment.

Am I trying to say we should always act in a manner that will bring joy to others at the expense of ourselves? No, I am not. I am trying to say that we should act in a manner that increases the *sum total* of joy in the world, and often that means we act in our own best interests. How do we decide? You already know the answer to that, you have always known.

When we look at the world as children, we do it with a sense of awe and admiration. Somehow, without anyone telling us, we sense that there is a connection between living things. We do not know yet that we share varying amounts of DNA with every single plant, animal, and human being on earth, we just know that we feel "comfortable" here, and we belong. Over the years we lose that sense of connection. As addicts, we do not feel comfortable in our own skins, let alone as inhabitants of earth.

When we start realizing again that we *are* connected, that every atom in everything we see was forged in the belly of a star, we begin to see ourselves as a part of a larger whole. We also see that when we treat others badly, we know it, and we pay the price in an increased level of stress. If we treat others well, we are treating ourselves well, and decreasing the sum total of misery in the world.

Know what you don't know

Very early in 1991, I attended my first AA conference. The keynote speaker was an elderly gentleman named Lou M., from Knoxville, Tennessee. Lou had been 12-stepped on the streets of New York City in 1940 by Ebby Thatcher, the fellow who first brought what later became the AA program to Bill Wilson. In fact, Bill became Lou's first AA sponsor. Lou received his 50-year medallion at that convention, making him a true AA pioneer.

I wanted to learn the "big secret" of how to stay sober so I could dispense with AA, and go on with my life. What better source was there to learn the "secret" from than someone who had been around as long as Lou had? I met him briefly in the midst of a crowd of people on Friday night, but had no time to speak to him alone. I rose early Saturday morning and waylaid the venerable gentleman in the midst of his morning walk.

After a little polite small talk, I asked him directly what the "most important" thing was in AA. If you could only keep one principle, one idea, one philosophy out of the whole program, what would it be? He didn't answer me right away. He thought about it, and I believe, took into consideration things he might have heard me say at a meeting the night before. Finally, after what seemed to be an eternity, he turned to me and said, "Pete, I think the most important thing is to know what you don't know."

What! That's it? Was that the best the old fool could do? He did not choose to elaborate, and I didn't probe any further. We resumed our walk, and I was left with what I thought was nothing but meaningless psychobabble.

Perhaps many of you already understand what he was talking about, but it took me several days to get there. I had to see a couple of things first. One of them was recognizing that most of the time at meetings I was a condescending jerk, who came across as someone who believed that he was the only "real" person in the room. I was quick to pick up addiction buzzwords, and reuse them without understanding what they meant or how they should be applied. I had to be the world's greatest expert on everything because I didn't believe anyone would like me if I wasn't.

If I didn't know something I would make it up. Lying always came easily to me, and of course my using exacerbated it. I always had to cover my butt with wife, employer, and others, and lying was how I did it. I wish I could say that it stopped the moment I quit drinking, but that would be another lie, and I am through doing that.

One day shortly after that conference I walked into a room full of people, and it occurred to me that every single person in that room knew something that I did not know. It did not matter what their background was, how much education they had, or how old they were, everyone knew something that I didn't know.

There was Mike over there who couldn't put a week

together without drinking, and never rose above carpenter's helper. He could build a doghouse without a plan; I couldn't. David, the painter, never finished grammar school, but he could look at a house and tell to the pint how much paint he would need. Mary, the twenty-year-old over in the corner, had spent three years on the street but was back in college, and knew more about literature than I ever did. It went on and on, it was horrible!

Not really, but it *was* new information. I had learned that it was okay not to know something, and that as human beings, we all have something worthwhile to communicate—even me. I didn't *know* this, and what's worse, I didn't *know* I didn't know. The whole concept of not knowing I didn't know something was foreign to me. There were certain things I thought I knew that I did not know very much about at all.

Do you know the best way to find out whether you truly know something or just think you know? Try to explain it to someone, or even to yourself. You do not even have to get really technical. Just pick a simple device outside of your areas of expertise. For instance, how does a refrigerator work? How about a toilet or a simple pump, how do they work? Can you explain to someone how a zipper works? In every poll, at least half of the voting population of the United States cannot name the three branches of government or what their responsibilities are, and yet we all think we know how to fix it.

We hear buzzwords and repeat them thinking we understand what they mean, when actually they mask gaps in our knowledge. We use them to gloss over concepts we do not fully understand. A prime contributor to the market crash of 2007 was a profound misunderstanding on the part of the finance industry of the true nature of the complex products they were selling to each other.

The problems come when we think we understand things when we do not, leading us to make decisions based upon inadequate knowledge. When you instruct someone, you have to fill the gaps in your own knowledge to explain the subject. Explain concepts to yourself as you learn them. Get in the habit of self-teaching.

When you uncover these gaps treat them as learning opportunities, not as signs of weakness. Success in recovery and in life rests on the assumption that you understand the problems you face. Sometimes, uncovering the flaw in that assumption will help you find a solution.

Think critically

Human beings evolved over thousands of years, adapting to the environment of the African savanna. There was a reproductive advantage to obeying the orders of older, wiser members of the tribe. Instructions like "don't swim with the alligators," and "don't go wandering from the camp at night," were expected to be obeyed without question. Young humans who obeyed these restrictions were more likely to reach puberty and reproduce than others, so the tendency to obey authority became dominant in our gene pool.

This tendency begins to disappear sometime around puberty, as every parent knows, and the adolescent begins to make more of their own decisions. Children tend to see the world as black or white, good or bad, while adolescents see the world through more complicated lenses. They are more likely to question the assertions of parents or society, and are less likely to accept what we tell them as absolute truth. These are healthy developments of course, and if properly directed can lead to the establishment of critical thinking skills. Unfortunately, our culture seems geared more towards teaching our young people *what* to think rather than *how* to think.

This brief section is not a course in critical thinking skills. I just want to introduce the idea that there *is* something called critical thinking, and learning a little about it will enhance your ability to use the cognitive techniques in this book. If you wish to go further in the study of critical thinking, a good place to start is this Critical Thinking Community web site: http://criticalthinking.org.

A commonly accepted definition of critical thinking is that presented by Michael Scriven and Richard Paul at the eighth Annual International Conference on Critical Thinking and Education Reform, in the summer of 1987:

> *"Critical thinking is the intellectually disciplined process of actively and skillfully conceptualizing, applying, analyzing, synthesizing and/or evaluating information gathered from, or generated by, observation, experience, reflection, reasoning, or communication, as a guide to belief and action."* [55]

Quite a mouthful, but what critical thinking encourages us to do is question not only the clarity and accuracy of our thinking, but also the depth and breadth. Not just considering if our "facts" are correct, but also if we are taking all of the alternatives into account. Is the content we are using relevant, and is our thinking process logical. In other words, using critical thinking skills forces us to think about our thinking.

Critical thinking enjoins us to ask questions about our thinking and beliefs:

- What do I think/believe about this?
- Why do I think/believe that?
- What is my knowledge/belief based upon?
- How am I viewing it?
- Should it (or can it) be viewed differently?

For years, we never questioned the thinking or beliefs that perpetuated our addictions. Now that we are trying to quit, we can and we must, if we are to recover successfully. Unless we challenge our old ideas and begin to look at the world from a different perspective, recovery will be difficult, if not impossible. That last question above is especially important because it is very difficult to change a belief unless we first change our point-of-view.

As students, and later as adults, we were rewarded for the ability to simply memorize and recall information. In most workplaces today, thinking "out of the box" is neither encouraged nor appreciated. From the media and society in general comes a constant barrage of messages, telling us what to think and believe about almost any conceivable subject. It is no wonder that many of us never learned to think critically. Actually, it is a miracle that we can think at all.

It is a good bet that before you picked up this book you accepted the majority non-professional view that addiction is a disease, addicts are powerless over it, and no one can recover without help. I have given you information here that should allow you to look at this dogma critically, and decide for yourself what is true and what is not. The studies I reference in *Powerless* are available for anyone to study, and you should. You should not take my view, or anyone's view, as the absolute truth without researching the questions to the best of your ability. That is the whole point of critical thinking—informed, logical decision-making.

I would like to introduce you to a popular problem-solving model called the *Six Steps to Effective Thinking and Problem Solving,* or "IDEALS" [56]

The IDEALS are to Identify, Define, Enumerate, Analyze, List, and Self-Correct:

- **Identify** the problem: *What is the real question we are facing?* Often, the belief that is causing our problem or anxiety is hiding under one or several surface thoughts, emotions, or beliefs. Solving the underlying problem or changing the underlying belief will often solve the others as well.

- **Define** the Context: *What are the facts that frame this problem?* Separate the real from the imaginary, the truth from the fiction, and the fact from the preconceived notion. This is often the most important step because we cannot solve our problems in the same frame of mind we used to create them.

- **Enumerate** the Choices: *What are the plausible options?* Brainstorm, by yourself or with the help of others. Consider everything possible, especially things you have not tried before.

- **Analyze** the Options: *What is the best course of action?* Do a Cost Benefit Analysis, or perhaps several on the various options. Consider each from all possible angles to arrive at the best solution.

- **List** Reasons Explicitly: *Why is this the best course of action?* Which option did you choose and why? If the solution does not work, it may be that one of your premises was wrong; this list will help you come to a new conclusion.

- **Self-Correct:** *Look at it again...what did I miss?* Before you put the plan into motion, check it again. Also, build a checkpoint into the plan where you will revisit it and re-evaluate your solution. Does it still fit the facts, and is the plan still viable?

This has been a short introduction to critical thinking. I encourage you to visit the web sites noted in this section for more information. Our recovery is only as good as the decisions we make.

Last

This is the last section of the text, and the shortest. I tried to be as up-to-date as possible, but our knowledge of addiction is expanding so rapidly that I am sure there are new developments that you should be aware of. During the four years that I have been researching and writing *Powerless,* I have had to rewrite some sections because of new advances.

There are some links in the Appendix that will give you a place to start looking for new data. The good news is that you are not powerless over your addiction; the bad news is that you are therefore responsible for your own recovery. The *Powerless* website has further information and some additional links.

The tools in *Powerless* are not "steps" to be taken one at

a time in sequential order; they will not work that way. We have to maintain our motivation, deal with urges, solve problems, *and* work towards lifestyle balance simultaneously to achieve stable recovery. We do not have to master all four at the beginning, we just have to be aware how they work together.

I hope that you have found something in these pages that will aid in your recovery. That is my part; the rest is up to you....

Appendix

References

Chapter 1

1. http://www.addictioninfo.org/articles/1587/1/Estimates-of-AAs-Effectiveness/Page1.html

Chapter 2

2. American Psychiatric Association, 1994. Diagnostic and Statistical Manual of Mental Disorders: DSM-IV. Washington D.C.: American Psychiatric Association. (pp. 181-183).

3. http://www.drugabuse.gov/publications/research-reports/tobacco-addiction/nicotine-addictive

4. Chapman S, MacKenzie R (2010) The Global Research Neglect of Unassisted Smoking Cessation: Causes and Consequences. PLoS Med 7(2): e1000216. doi:10.1371/journal.pmed.1000216

5. http://ajph.aphapublications.org/cgi/reprint/97/8/1503.pdf

6. http://www.cfah.org/hbns/archives/viewSupportDoc.cfm?supportingDocID=522

7. Chapman S, MacKenzie R (2010) The Global Research Neglect of Unassisted Smoking Cessation: Causes and Consequences. PLoS Med 7(2): e1000216. doi:10.1371/journal.pmed.1000216

8. Gillies V, Willig C (1997) You get the nicotine and that in your blood: constructions of addiction and control in women's accounts of cigarette smoking. J Community Appl Soc Psychol 7:285-301

9. Winick, C. (1962). Maturing out of narcotic addiction. *Bulletin on Narcotics, 14*(1), 1-7

10. Drew, L. R. H. (1968). Alcoholism as a self-limiting disease. *Quarterly Journal of Studies on Alcohol,* 29, 956-967

11. Robins, L. N., Davis, D.H., & Goodwin, D.W. (1974), Drug use by Army enlisted men in Vietnam: A follow-up on their return home. *American Journal of Epidemiology, 99*, 235-

249

12. Robins, L.N., Helzer, J.E., & Davis, D.H. (1975) Narcotic use in Southeast Asia and afterwards: An interview study of 898 Vietnam returnees. *Archives of General Psychiatry, 32,* 955-961.

13. Robins, L.N. (1993) Vietnam veterans' rapid recovery from heroin addiction: A fluke or normal expectation? *Addiction, 88,* 1041-1054

14. Hasin, D.S., & Grant, B.F. (1995). AA and other help seeking for alcohol problems: Former drinkers in the US general population. *Journal of Substance Abuse, 7,* 281-292

15. Sobell, L.C. Cunningham, J.A., & Sobell, M.B. (1996) Recovery from alcohol problems with and without treatment: Prevalence in two population surveys. *American Journal of Public Health,7* 966-972

16. Dawson D.A. et al (2005) Recovery from DSM-IV alcohol dependence: United States 2001-2002 *Addiction, 100* 281-292

17. Cunningham J.A., Lin, E., Ross, H.E., & Walsh, G.W. (2000). Factors associated with untreated remission from alcohol abuse or dependence. *Addictive Behaviors, 25* 317-321

18. Schutte, K.K., Moos, R.H., & Brennan, P.L. (2006). Predictors of untreated remission from late-life drinking problems. *Journal of Studies on Alcohol, 67* 354-362.

19. Sobell, L.C., Ellingstad, T.P., & Sobell, M.B. (2000) Natural recovery from alcohol and drug problems: Methodological review of the research with suggestions for future directions. *Addiction, 95,* 749-764

20. Sobell, L.C., Ellingstad, T.P., & Sobell, M.B. (2000) Natural recovery from alcohol and drug problems: Methodological review of the research with suggestions for future directions. *Addiction, 95,* 749-764

21. Breslin, F.C., et al. (1997). Alcohol treatment outcome methodology: State of the art 1989-1993. *Addictive Behaviors, 22*(2), 145-155

22. Rosenberg, H. (1993) Prediction of controlled drinking by

alcoholics and problem drinkers. *Psychological Bulletin, 113*, 129-139*Bulletin, 113*, 129-139

Chapter 3

23. Chaney, W. 2006. *Workbook for a dynamic mind. Las Veges, Houghton_Brace Publishing, pg 44*

24. *Gopnik, A, Meltzoff, A.N., & Kuhl, P.K. 1999.* The scientist in the crib: Minds, brains and how children learn. New York: William Morrow, P. 181

25. Ibid

26. Robertson, I.H., & Murre, J.M.J. 1999. Rehabilitation of brain damage: Brain plasticity and principles of guided recovery. *Psychological Bulletin, 125,*

27. Wilson, W.A.,&Kuhn, C.M. 2005 *How addiction hijacks our reward system.* Cerebrum: The Dana Forum on Brain Science Vol. 7, No. 2 pps 53-66

28. Evidenced based mindfulness: Research studies - http://www.fammed.wisc.edu/mindfulness/research

29. Kalivas, P.W., and O'Brien, C. 2008. *Drug Addiction as a Pathology of Staged Neuroplasticity.* Neuropsychopharmacology Reviews, 33, pg. 167

30. Wilson, W.A.&Kuhn, C.M. 2005. *How addiction hijacks our reward system.* Cerebrum: The Dana Forum on Brain Science Vol. 7, no. 2, pps 53-66

31. Kalivas, P.W., and O'Brien, C. 2008. *Drug Addiction as a Pathology of Staged Neuroplasticity.* Neuropsychopharmacology Reviews, 33, pg. 167

32. Kelley, A.E. 2004. *Memory and addiction: shared neural circuitry and molecular mechanisms.* Neuron 44: pps 161-179

33. Nestler, E.J. 2005 *Is there a common molecular pathway for addiction?* National Neuroscience 8: pps 1445-1449

34. Berridge, K., Robinson, T. 1998. *What is the role of dopamine in reward: hedonic impact, reward learning, or incentive salience?* Brain Research Reviews 28: pps 309-369

35. *How Addiction Hijacks the Brain.* Harvard Helpguide:

http://www.helpguide.org/harvard/addiction_hijacks_brain.
htm

36. Deutch, A.Y., Roth, R.H. 1990. *The determinants of stress-induced activation of the prefrontal cortical dopamine system.* Progressive Brain Research 85: pps 357-393

37. Kalivas, P.W., and O'Brien, C. 2008. *Drug Addiction as a Pathology   of   Staged   Neuroplasticity.* Neuropsychopharmacology Reviews, 33, pg. 168

38. Schultz, W. 2004. *Neural coding of basic reward terms of animal learning theory, game theory, microeconomics and behavioural ecology.* Current Opinion in Neurobiology 14: 139-147

39. Wilson, W.A.&Kuhn, C.M. 2005. *How addiction hijacks our reward system.* Cerebrum: The Dana Forum on Brain Science Vol. 7, no. 2, pps 53-66

40. Everitt, B.J., & Robbins, T.W. 2005 Neural systems of reinforcement for drug addiction: from action to habits to compulsion. *Nature Neuroscience: 8: 1481-1489*

41. Kolb, B. Et al. 2004. *Plasticity and functions of the orbital frontal cortex.* Brain and Cognitive Sciences 55: pps 104-115

42. Minerbi, A. Et al. 2009. *Long-term relationships between synaptic tenacity, synaptic remodeling and network activity.* Plos   Biology: http://willcov.com'bioconsciousness/sidebars/synaptic%20 remodeling.%20abd%20network%20activity.htm

Chapter 6

43. http://www.behaviortherapy.com/ResearchDiv/wh atworks.aspx

Chapter 7

44. http://www.orange-papers.org/orange-rroot030.html

45. http://www.sciencebasedmedicine.org/index.php/aa-is-faith-based-not-evidence-based/

46. http://lifeprocessprogram.com/lp-blog/how-to-fight-and-beat-addiction/

47. Alcoholics Anonymous (1939). Alcoholics Anonymous: The story of how many thousands of men and women have recovered from alcoholism. (New York. Alcoholics Anonymous World Services, Inc., 1976), 59.

48. Alcoholics Anonymous (1939). Alcoholics Anonymous: The story of how many thousands of men and women have recovered from alcoholism. (New York. Alcoholics Anonymous World Services, Inc., 1976), 84.

49. http://www.silkworth.net/freestuff.html

50. http://www.jmir.org/2013/7/e134/

Chapter 10

51. http://pubs.niaaa.nih.gov/publications/arcr344/432-440.htm

52. H. Harrington Cleveland, Kitty S. Harris. The role of coping in moderating within-day associations between negative triggers and substance use cravings: A daily diary investigation. Addictive Behaviors, 2010; 35 (1): 60 DOI: 10.1016/j.addbeh.2009.08.010

Chapter 11

53. Gorski, T. F., & Miller, M. (1982). Counseling for relapse prevention. Independence, MO:Herald House - Independence Press.

54. http://casaa.unm.edu/inst/Aware.pdf

Chapter 13

55. Scriven, M., & Paul, R. (2007). *Defining critical thinking.* The Critical Thinking Community: Foundation for Critical Thinking. Retrieved June 10, 2013, from HTTP://www.criticalthinking.org/aboutCT/define_critical_thinking.cfm

56. Facing, P.A. (2007). *Critical thinking: What it is and why it counts.* Retrieved June 10th, 2013, from HTTP://telacommunications.com/nutshell/cthinking7.htm

Resources

These are some additional sources of current information on addiction, and links to a few recovery group websites. These listings are not intended to be a complete list of what is available to you, but they should provide a starting point for further study. Some sites offer daily updates on the newest developments in the addiction field. Appearance on either of these lists does not necessarily constitute an endorsement, as I have tried to include a broad range of approaches. These links are in alphabetical order.

Addiction information links:

Addictioninfo.org, alternatives to 12-step treatment, is a website full of interesting information on many forms of addictions. This link is to a page on the website called *Natural Recovery From Addiction Beyond the 12 Steps:* http://www.addictioninfo.org/articles/2978/1/Natural-Recovery-From-Addiction-Beyond-the-12-Steps/Page1.html

Alcoholism isn't what it used to be, NIAAA Spectrum February, 2011. This is only one of the many excellent articles and papers in the Spectrum. http://www.spectrum.niaaa.nih.gov/features/alcoholism.aspx

Alcohol Reports is an international website dedicated to providing current information on news, reports, publications, and peer-reviewed research articles concerning alcoholism and alcohol-related problems throughout the world. Postings are provided by international contributors who monitor news, publications, and research findings in their country, geographical region, or program area of interest:

http://alcoholreports.blogspot.com

The National Institute on Alcohol Abuse and Alcoholism (NIAAA) offers timely scientific papers on alcoholism and other topics: http://www.niaaa.nih.gov/

Nicotine Addiction 101, from the pages of whyquit.com contains a good explanation of the process of addiction to a particular drug, in this case nicotine. Much of what they say is applicable to any drug, and they do a good job of debunking the nonsense from the nicotine replacement industry: http://whyquit.com/whyquit/LinksAAddiction.html

The Science Daily website covers the latest news in many fields of science. This link is to the *Addiction* page. If you sign up, they will send you updates whenever they publish new articles. If you wish to keep up with what's happening in the field, this is the place to do it: http://www.sciencedaily.com/news/mind_brain/addiction/

The Fix is an excellent site for news concerning all phases of addiction and recovery. They will send email updates on a periodic basis when they publish new articles. http://www.thefix.com/

Recovery website links:

The international website of *Alcoholics Anonymous*: http://www.aa.org

I mentioned *Moderation Management* in Chapter 7, as a possibility for those who would like to moderate their use of alcohol, rather than abstain. Here is their main website, and all of their program information: http://www.moderation.org/

Rational Recovery doesn't have any meetings; they offer an approach to recovery that is totally self-help. Their primary tool, which they call Addictive Voice Recognition Technique® or

AVRT® deals with that addictive voice in your head that tells you it's okay to use: https://rational.org/index.php?id=1

Recovery International uses the cognitive-behavioral, peer-to-peer self-help training system developed by Dr. Abraham Low. They have both face-to-face and online meetings. http://www.lowselfhelpsystems.org/

Secular Organizations for Sobriety (Save Our Selves) is part of the Center For Inquiry in Los Angeles. They have face-to-face meetings all over the world. They focus simply on making sobriety a number-one priority for recovering alcoholics. http://www.cfiwest.org/sos/index.htm

SMART Recovery® primarily uses Rational Emotive Behavior Therapy, a cognitive behavioral therapy developed by Dr. Albert Ellis. They offer meetings online and all over the world. http://smartrecovery.org/

Author Biography

Pete Soderman is a published author and lecturer, with a background in computer engineering and sales. He had a 26-year drinking career that began the day before the assassination of President Kennedy, and ended in 1990. Since then he has been helping others to recover, as a self-help facilitator, while staying abreast of the latest scientific advances in the addiction field. He lives on the shores of Lake Chapala, in central Mexico, with his wife, Gethyn. He can be reached at http://powerlessnolonger.com.

Index